# The Cemetery Traveler

Written, researched, and photographed

by

**Ed Snyder**

ISBN: 9781717885951

# *DEADICATION*

I began my *Cemetery Traveler* blog in order to share my decades-long experience with all things cemeterial. As a photographer specializing in images of cemetery statuary, I've run into some interesting people, had some unexplainable experiences, and had a lot of fun.

This book has been highly influential in its absence. Hundreds of people have commented on the individual blog postings on my Cemetery Traveler blog (https://thecemeterytraveler.blogspot.com/), and it feels good to know that people have appreciated what I've written. Starting out, I would never have guessed how much an ancestor's headstone could mean to a descendant. So many people need a tangible link to their past (which is one reason Ancestry.com has become so popular). As I write this introduction in 2018, I can say without a doubt that many more people have become interested in, and comfortable around, cemeteries since I began exploring them in 1997.

I certainly appreciate the time you're about to give me as I set the inner workings of my mind to print. Some refer to cemetery travel as dark tourism. Whatever you might call it – a sickness, an avocation, deadication, one thing is certain - the stories herein are like mirrors for me, windows to you - reflecting my soul to me while allowing you a glimpse inside. As for an actual dedication, I dedicate this book to all who came before us – we are better people because of your influence.

Link to The Cemetery Traveler blog:
**https://thecemeterytraveler.blogspot.com/**

**Other books by Ed Snyder:**

*Stone Angels* (Blurb)
http://www.blurb.com/b/574773-stone-angels

*Digital Photography for the Impatient* (Amazon)
https://www.amazon.com/Digital-Photography-Impatient-Ed-Snyder/dp/1448648270

**Ed Snyder's websites**:

http://www.edsnyderphoto.com/
http://www.stoneangels.net/

**Ed Snyder on social media:**

https://www.facebook.com/Ed-Snyders-StoneAngels-Photography-115216101833187/

https://www.instagram.com/mourningarts/?hl=en

**To purchase artwork:**

If you like the images you see in this book or on my websites, and would like to own a print, please contact me at mourningarts@yahoo.com
…or check what is available on my
ETSY store: https://www.etsy.com/shop/StoneAngels?ref=shop_sugg

# CONTENTS

# ACKNOWLEDGMENTS

I would like to acknowledge the many people who have read, subscribed to, and commented on my Cemetery Traveler blog. Throughout this book, I will include comments people have made from time to time. I truly appreciate your candor, humor, and insightfulness.

My blogs on the Internet are free, but this book costs money. So let me just say that I appreciate you buying this book. My family had great stories, but only passed them on via word of mouth. I begged my mother to write some things down after my Dad died. She complied, to a degree. I will not fall into that trap. No man shall say of me, when ghost I be, "he should have written this down!"

Lastly, I want to acknowledge the fact that my interest in cemeteries began by wanting to photograph them. Everything else sprang from that.

*"Your photos make me wish I was dead (I mean that in a good way)."*

–Randall R.

# SECTION 1:

# POISONING THE WELL

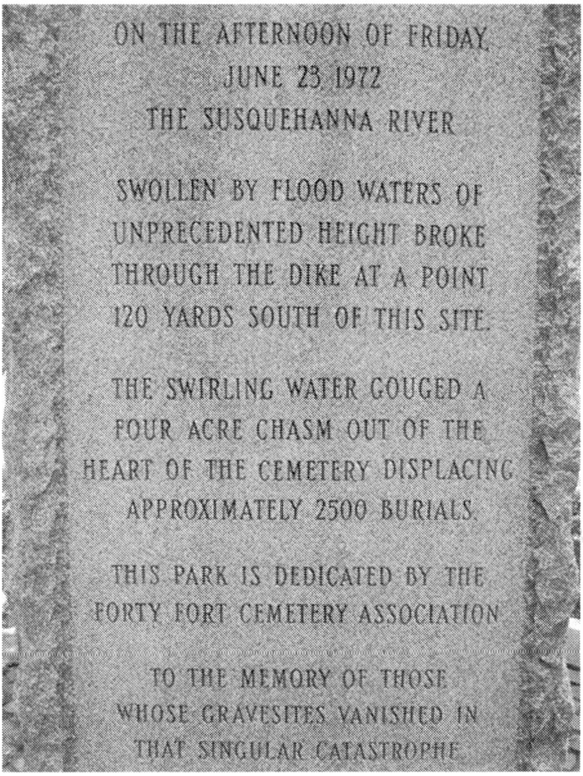


The passage you are about to read will serve as an introduction, of sorts, to this book of selections from my Cemetery Traveler blog (https://thecemeterytraveler.blogspot.com/). I began writing the blog in 2010, as a natural extension of the previous ten years I had spent photographing cemeteries across the U.S. and Europe. People frequently ask me why I do this. My assumption is that it has something to do with the following experience. Or it may just be a flaw in my personality.

(The actual introduction to this book will come a bit later, when I think you're ready for it.)

**2,000 caskets washed away, body parts were deposited on roofs, porches … and in basements."**
(https://en.wikipedia.org/wiki/Hurricane_Agnes)

The headline above was the catalyst for my fascination with cemeteries, I believe. I can almost pinpoint it to the day, maybe June 30, 1972, this event that so poisoned the well. I was thirteen years old (seems fitting, right?). Hurricane Agnes hit the east coast of the United States in June of that year, and my young world changed in many ways. I had never lived through a "disaster" before. My parents' home was flooded and the entire first floor destroyed by eight feet of water from the Susquehanna River. This happened in the northeastern part of Pennsylvania, with our largest local city, Wilkes–Barre, receiving the lion's share of the "Wrath of Agnes," as it came to be known.

As a kid, I didn't consider that I, personally, lost much, since everything in my bedroom on the second floor of the house was untouched. My chemistry set, my electric guitar, my record albums. The entire first floor of the house was destroyed, however. I found it hard to get excited over the loss of kitchen appliances. I might have been a little riled that this happened in the summer, however, obliterating my school vacation.

One thing that WAS exciting, however, was the fact that the swollen river broke through the dikes at the site of the Forty–Fort Cemetery, in the town of Forty–Fort, PA. This was about two miles from where I lived in Luzerne. As a result of the break, forty–eight square miles and almost 30,000 residences and commercial properties were inundated by flood waters on both sides of the river. About 100,000 people were evacuated. No small event, this.

## Five Feet High and Rising

A day or so before the dike broke through, the river was close to overflowing its banks. "Five feet high an' risin,'" as Johnny Cash sang on my father's portable record player. Actually, the river crested a bit over forty feet – four feet above the city's levees (dikes), flooding downtown Wilkes–Barre itself with nine feet of water.

Most of the day on June 23, 1972, scores of volunteers sandbagged on the dike in front of my grandmother's house in Kingston. By afternoon, the rising river blew up out of the street storm drains like geysers. This caused some minor flooding in the streets of the towns, but it wasn't enough to equalize the water pressure. As a result, the twenty–foot high dike at the Forty–Fort Cemetery blew out. Not only was the Wyoming Valley under about nine feet of water for days, but the cemetery was gutted.

**2,700 graves were displaced. Only about half of them were found.**

While my parents, brother, sister and I were staying on high ground with my aunt and uncle, we would hear news reports of the bodies and caskets that had washed out of the cemetery. Rumors ran that unearthed coffins had rushed down Wyoming Avenue and became lodged onto the front porches of peoples' homes (I do remember seeing news photos of such scenes just after the flood). At the time, the Victorian–era Forty–Fort Cemetery was an active burial ground (meaning that there had continually been new burials since its establishment in 1869). Which means, of course, that some of the unearthed coffins and body parts may have been relatively fresh.

After the flood waters receded, people were slowly allowed back to their homes – or what was left of them. Some homes were completely washed away. We stayed with my aunt and uncle for about a week and a half – from evacuation to readmittance. Martial Law had been declared while the U.S. Army Corps of Engineers and Civil Defense cleared streets, removed giant trees from the roofs of peoples' homes, and boarded up the cemetery. The latter, I assumed, was done after all the coffins, skeletons, and other remains had been collected. Turns out that the collected remains were re–interred in a suburban cemetery, miles away (on higher ground). A groundskeeper told me in 2016 that his grandfather was the caretaker of the cemetery when the flood came. He said burial records were lost as well.

*"On the afternoon of Friday*
*June 23, 1972*
*the Susquehanna River*
*swollen by flood waters of*
*unprecedented height broke*
*through the dike at a point*
*120 yards south of this site."*
– Inscribed on the monument in the center of the Forty–Fort Cemetery

One of the first things I did after being allowed back onto the flood plain was visit this source of macabre facts and fables, the Forty–Fort Cemetery. My cousin Albert and I walked the dike from our grandmother's house (which had also been flooded, but not destroyed) north to Forty–Fort, a distance of about a mile. Walking the dike was easier on the eyes and lungs than walking along the roadways. The streets were dusty with flood mud, which had baked for days in the hot summer sun. Huge clouds of tan dust fowled the air, kicked up by cars and trucks.

When we arrived, we could see that the old iron fence along Wyoming Avenue and River Street had received a layer of eight–foot high plywood. This blocked the view to the inside of the cemetery. Not easily deterred (and driven by some morbid fascination I don't quite understand), we found a dugout below the fence near the cemetery's meetinghouse on River Street. Kind of looked like a dog was responsible for this excavation (I cringe as I write this – you'll soon see why). With some difficulty, Albert and I squirmed our way under the fence, on our backs.

Why the plywood kept the stench inside the cemetery baffles me to this day. When I stood upright inside, the smell nearly knocked me out. It was overpowering, not of this world. We had to breathe through our mouths the whole time we were there. This amounted to no more than about twenty minutes, really, but that was enough. I've been curious about death, burials, and cemeteries ever since.

Until I began "The Cemetery Traveler" blog in 2010, I really didn't write much about my experiences in cemeteries. I explored cemeteries all over the United States with my camera for about ten years prior to starting the blog. I didn't really understand at the time why I was doing all this. As I began putting my blogs together to create this book, it dawned on me that my experience in the Forty–Fort Cemetery must have been a cathartic moment, of sorts. I never wrote about my actual experience in the cemetery to this extent. But back to what we saw.

The force of the water tossed gravestones about like toys and destroyed three granite mausoleums. Large trees were uprooted, as were coffins and concrete burial vaults. – *The Wrath of Agnes* (Media Affiliates, Inc., Wilkes–Barre, Pa 1972).

Inside the cemetery, there were huge gouges in the earth, holes gobbling down Victorian–era granite monuments and expelling coffins. We walked the distance between the front of the cemetery on Wyoming Avenue to the rear of the property, where the dike had been dramatically swept away. "A whirlpool of tremendous force" had torn out the levee's pilings and an eight to ten foot wall of water came rushing into the cemetery, according to the book, *The Wrath of Agnes* (Media Affiliates, Inc., Wilkes–Barre, Pa 1972).

We could not, at the time, comprehend the magnitude of the devastation. I remember being surprised to see wooden coffins lying about, intermingled with fancier metal ones. I suppose I thought the older ones would have disintegrated. Though the cemetery had been around since 1869, this moist earth so close to the river must have preserved the old pine boxes – and their contents – quite well. Concrete burial vaults were sticking out of the ground. Gold and silver–colored metal caskets were resting on the ground, their lids open. They were empty. Some of them, I found out later, had been retrieved from around the town. Loose bones had likely been either collected or nabbed by dogs.

I'm sure we kept up some kind of boisterous chatter, Albert and I, just to make each other believe we were not scared. Albert was only a year older than I. Neither of us had ever been this close to death. The ground was solid, so we weren't sinking in mud. We had to walk around the many holes all around us. The river at the cemetery's edge was low and muddy. Acres upon acres of destruction, like a gruesome landfill. Later, the disinterred coffins along with the remains of 1400 bodies would be buried in a mass grave in some other cemetery, and a memorial marker erected here in Forty–Fort Cemetery, their original resting place.

*"The swirling water gouged a*
*four acre chasm out of the*
*heart of the cemetery displacing*
*approximately 2500 burials."*
– Inscribed on the monument in the center of the Forty–Fort Cemetery

I suppose it was too difficult to install temporary fencing along the areas where the dike had washed away, at the back of the cemetery. As a result, there was easy access to the property if you approached it from the river. We knew that other people had been in the cemetery before us. It had been a week since the caskets and body parts were retrieved and several days after the Army put up the plywood. As we approached the river to head home, we were startled by evidence of a prior explorer. This geographic area is largely rural and blue collar. Lots of deer hunting goes on here, both rifle as well as archery.

As we approached what was left of the dike, I turned around to take a last look at the devastation. What I saw froze my blood. Propped up against a large tree, facing the river, was a wooden coffin, sans lid. A female corpse lay inside. Its arms were crossed across its chest and she wore a black lace dress. While there was still flesh on the bones, her face had the dry look of mummification. Below her arms, sticking out of her torso, were three hunting arrows. Target practice for some local yokel.

Albert threw up. I was in shock. We hadn't seen the corpse upon our approach, as the coffin was propped up against the side of the tree facing away from us. We had walked right past it. I don't remember what I thought about this at the time. It was all simply too much stimuli bombarding my senses simultaneously. Disrespect for the dead did not enter my young mind. None of the Hammer horror films my father took us to see at the drive–ins in the sixties prepared me for that sight. A visual like that can stay with you awhile—like, for the rest of your life.

*"This park is dedicated by the*
*Forty Fort Cemetery Association*
*to the memory of those*
*whose gravesites vanished in*
*that singular catastrophe."*
– Inscribed on the monument in the center of the Forty–Fort Cemetery

Now there is a large granite memorial in the center of the Forty–Fort Cemetery, to remember the estimated 2,700 graves were displaced. Most of the recovered remains were reburied elsewhere. Somewhere out there, the remains of the remaining 1,300 bodies still lie nestled in rural woods, streams, and very bad dreams. The gaping wound in the center of the cemetery caused by the flooding whirlpool was later filled in with dirt and rock. It is now an open field with a large granite memorial at its center. Burials ceased after the flood, but endowments apparently allow for the grounds to be meticulously cared for, an ongoing example of our respect for the dead – the dead who were not allowed to rest in peace.

## Epilogue

At the beginning of this story, you see a photograph I made of the memorial in 2014. I did not have a camera with me during my 1972 visit. Certain memories, however, leave indelible after–images. I still do not understand my initial morbid fascination with that cemetery disaster. However, I believe the event did plant a seed that much later grew into a healthy fascination with cemeteries, and with death in general.

I did not return to the Forty–Fort Cemetery for about thirty–five years. I actually left the region in 1979 when I graduated college and moved away. My family still lives in the area, and I visit a few times each year. In 2014, I visited the Forty–Fort Cemetery. I supposed by that time I had enough cemetery travel experience under my belt to face up to my old fears. I had begun writing The Cemetery Traveler blog in 2010 and had published about forty essays at that point. I had visited hundreds of cemeteries across the U.S. and even one in Italy. The Forty–Fort Cemetery is like no other. The tree is still there. Unmistakably, this was the tree against which the wooden coffin stood. The meetinghouse was still in the same location, and I could tell where the dugout had been under the old black iron fence. As I trod the moist earth, seeping up from the Susquehanna River, I partly disagreed with Heraclitus, who said that you cannot step into the same river twice. I felt like I had stepped back into the exact same river.

**References:**

http://www.fortyfortmeetinghouse.org/cemetery.html:
https://search.yahoo.com/yhs/search?p=forty+fort+cemetery+hurricane+agnes&ei=UTF-8&hspart=mozilla&hsimp=yhs-001
https://petejoem.files.wordpress.com/2014/02/agnes2.jpg
http://www.accuweather.com/en/weather-news/flood-victims-agnes-1972/66825
http://www.accuweather.com/en/outdoor-articles/outdoor-living/hurricane-agnes-photo-gallery/66779
(https://www.washingtonpost.com/blogs/capital-weather-gang/post/hurricane-agnes-a-look-back-after-40-years/2012/06/21/gJQAnDS0sV_blog.html?noredirect=on&utm_term=.fa7fa8967fed )
(https://en.wikipedia.org/wiki/Hurricane_Agnes)
Final Report of the Disaster Survey Team on the Events of Agnes (U.S. DEPARTMENT OF COMMERCE, Feb. 1973)
https://www.gpo.gov/fdsys/pkg/CZIC-qc877-n3-no-73-1/html/CZIC-qc877-n3-no-73-1.htm

# SECTION 2:

# THE ALLURE OF THE ABANDONED GRAVEYARD

—Abandoned, Forgotten, Neglected

The abandoned graveyard, to me, was for the longest time, an enigma. As it is for many. "How," people ask me, "do cemeteries become 'abandoned?'" The answer is probably different for every one of the many abandoned graveyards in existence. How a cemetery becomes abandoned is probably less an event than a process. Mismanagement and criminal intent are certainly options that have been exercised in the past. But other things happen too. Graveyards get filled up, and with no new burials, there is no income to maintain the property. Owners then, perhaps, disappear. Unless some conscientious individuals feel it is incumbent on them to step in and help, the property may be condemned and destroyed. Paved over. Perhaps with the bodies still in the ground.

Intrigued by the genre, I explore abandoned and neglected graveyards whenever and wherever possible. My hope is to shed light (and public awareness) on them before their inhabitants become lost to history, and their memorials are ravaged by the artillery of time (to borrow a phrase from Abe Lincoln).

*"The dead absolutely talk to us. On 2 different occasions, when trying to locate graves of loved ones, I walked up and down the rows repeatedly, to no avail. Each time, frustrated and ready to give up, I made one last attempt, beseeching the ancestor to please help me find them. Each time, they stopped me at the row they were in, and then again at their grave. Creepy? Nope. They wanted me to find them."* – Karen B.

# Christmas in the Cemetery

Originally published Friday, December 24, 2010

https://thecemeterytraveler.blogspot.com/2010/12/christmas-in-cemetery.html

Know what Christmas and photographing cemetery statuary have in common? No? …. Well neither do I. But suddenly, its Christmas, and I feel the need to connect the two. Sure, I could use Angels as the crossover vehicle, but that would be like shooting fish in a barrel. Christmas decorations in cemeteries are generally sad and depressing —I needed something edgier.

I was talking with my Mom recently and I guess because it's close to Christmas she launched into a story about how much she enjoyed taffy pulls and plum pudding as a child at her grandmother's house. Her grandparents were Welsh coal miners and celebrated Christmas in traditional ways, playing dominoes and Chinese Checkers, enjoying family. I never knew them, unfortunately — they all died off before and during my early childhood. I picture her as one of the children in Dylan Thomas' 1954 poem, 'A Child's Christmas in Wales.' He writes of the relations who ate Christmas dinner together, napped, and drank elderberry wine.

Perhaps the connection between cemeteries and Christmas is that the people in my mother's story, as well as in Thomas' poem, are long dead. Friends have died as well—kids I knew and played pond hockey with—fell through the ice and drowned. Thomas writes about small boys, though warned, who skated on the frozen pond drowned.

Not having any particular talent for marrying an assortment of disparate topics together in any sort of cogent narrative, I decided to temporarily shelve this blog. While I usually wear my limitations with pride, I believe, like Keats, that if writing doesn't come as naturally as leaves to a tree, it ought not to come at all. So instead of forcing myself to continue, I put it aside, for some days, until the ending ceased to elude me.

And we're back. That didn't take long, now did it? (Like writer's block must not take long for Stephen King.) To get the incubus of this story off my chest, I drove out to my favorite abandoned cemetery and realized that what I REALLY want for Christmas is snow! I want to see the tombstones and mausoleums in this godforsaken overgrown forest of a cemetery, in Thomas' muffling silence of eternal snows. What a wonderful decoration that would be!

Snow, a metaphor for purity, always adds a layer of beguiling beauty over the ground, like pancake makeup on the face of an old carney clown. Such a pall would cover the dumped loads of building materials, tines, the mattresses and church pews. It may add some adventure as you step through the snow only to smash through some discarded stained glass window or bag of garbage. But all this can only add to the experience. Snow is magical and theatrical at the same time —it would cap and clothe the broken limbed cemetery angels and hide our indiscretions.

In such a winter wonderland, the abandoned cemetery may not seem such a sad place. Like a veil hiding the sins of stolen cars and illegal burials, the snow would make the sordid appear normal, innocent, and clean. The feral cats and wild pit bulls would either adapt, or die. The cats turning into polar felines gliding through the drifts, like the ones Thomas describes as he waits to snowball them. One wonders where the feral pit bulls have gone for the winter? Maybe the turkey vultures got them.

I write this as an old friend emails me and tells me he's having brain surgery in two days, and may not make it. Back yonder, I wasn't sure how to end this story. Be careful what you wish for. The regret I have is not seeing him as often as I should have, like the regret of not having made the effort to save an abandoned cemetery. Ironic in that the purpose of a cemetery is to help us remember people. When we desert a cemetery, we desert our own history. Do we fear the ghosts of our past so much? Our society is not as apt to pave a cemetery as it is to raze an historic building, which is good. The result is that in many cases, the cemetery is simply abandoned. Better that it be forgotten than lost to history, however, because then there is still hope for recovery. Unlike people with terminal illness, "things" can be stabilized and restored, regardless of their condition. That's when it occurred to me—what better way to bring attention to urban blight in need of healing than to light up this old forgotten dump of a cemetery with Christmas Lights! A cause célèbre! If I had the wherewithal, I'd buy a diesel generator, tow it here, and use it to power thousands of big, old–fashioned Christmas lights that I would string from the peaks and eaves of the old mausoleums!

Wait, I know what you're thinking—that I'm writing this on my day pass from the asylum. But think of it! With snow falling, standing in the center of a circle of decrepit old tombs, faux dwellings illuminated by joyous lights strung from one to the other, like so many South Philly rowhomes! The mausoleums built on the high ridge here are about the only structures you can see from the parkway — imagine the drivers slowing down to look! Imagine this circle of mournfully extravagant, blocked up and grafittied memorials awash in falling snow—a funereal snowglobe of emotion that would draw everyone's attention to mortality, and possibly encourage us to respectfully treat each other as equals, or as Dickens put it, fellow passengers to the grave.

This Christmas I think of all the familiar voices that have fallen silent in my life, whose lives have vanished and become no more than a dream. This once–grand Victorian cemetery that boasted inhabitants of consequence, now rots in peace. Its residents no more heeded than angels with broken wings. Maybe the Jews have the right idea, avoiding "guardian angels" in their funerary art. A cracked angel is a forlorn sight, and makes one even more sullen when seen in the midst of such squalor. I once asked a Jewish friend of mine why there are no angels in Jewish cemeteries. She humorously answered, "They would interfere with our suffering."

I've just seen the weather report—it's supposed to snow on Christmas! I'll dream about abandoned mausoleums strung with Christmas lights, to illuminate the memory of people we've lost, those we've forgotten, and folks we've never known. I would like to light up Dylan Thomas' close and holy darkness. Merry Christmas, everyone.

# The Watery Remains of Monument Cemetery

Originally published Saturday, April 30, 2011

https://thecemeterytraveler.blogspot.com/2011/04/watery-remains-of-monument-cemetery.html

Normally, I don't find myself checking tide tables before going on a photographic excursion to a cemetery. But when my friend Leo and I decided to search for underwater tombstones from Philadelphia's defunct Monument Cemetery, we needed to heed the table, as most of the stones are covered at high tide. No, this is not of one of those offshore cemeteries in a coral reef – nothing quite so romantic. These are the remains of Monument Cemetery, Philadelphia's largest vanished Victorian graveyard.

**Off–shore burial?**

So my cemetery travels have taken me this time not to an actual cemetery, but to the Delaware River waterfront under the Betsy Ross Bridge (Philadelphia side), where the remains of this once grand Victorian cemetery lie. In this secluded, wooded area, scores of granite headstones, monuments, and ironwork lie on the shore, protrude from the embankment, and peek out of the murky river water.

Friday, April 22, 2011

| | Tide Time | Height Feet | Sunrise Sunset | Moon | Time |
|---|---|---|---|---|---|
| Low | 12:13 AM | 0.6 | 6:13 AM | Rise | 12:11 AM |
| High | 5:43 AM | 7.6 | 7:45 PM | Set | 9:43 AM |
| Low | 12:57 PM | 0.4 | | | |
| High | 6:21 PM | 6.6 | | | |

http://www.saltwatertides.com/cgi–local/neatlantic.cgi

**How did tombstones get in the river?**

I'd originally read about the demise of Monument Cemetery in Tom Keels' book, Philadelphia Graveyards and Cemeteries (Arcadia Publishing, 2003), but I still thought it might be an urban legend. When I read in his "Vanished Cemeteries" chapter that the monuments and grave markers were dumped into the river and you can see them sticking out of the water at low tide, I knew I had to check this out personally. At my request, Tom graciously gave me quite specific directions to get there, adding:
"… this is a fairly desolate, industrial area. Please take all precautions – go with one or two people during the daytime, bring your cell phone, and be on the alert. "

As with any attempt at urban exploration, you need to be prepared — hiking shoes, tough clothes, weapons. You never know what kind of nutters you'll run into — members of the transient community, kids having beer parties, ne'er–do–wells. But success only comes to those who brass it out.
So after some months of planning and reading other people's accounts of their treks to the riverfront (some successful, some not), I figured out when low tide would occur and enlisted my friend Leo to come along. As it turned out, access to the riverfront is made near the intersection of Delaware and Castor Avenues, in the Bridesburg section of Philadelphia, right between an abandoned power plant and an active industrial complex.

The power plant was actually the site of my first official urban exploration excursion with a group of experienced explorers. At the last minute, I chickened out. It just seemed too risky – I'd already been arrested once for trespassing. The aborted power plant experience paid off, however, in that the vicinity was now familiar to me – the dumped gravestones from Monument Cemetery were at the same riverfront area, only on the opposite side of a canal.

## The Demise of Monument Cemetery

Monument Cemetery in Philadelphia (located at North Broad and Berks streets), was the city's second Victorian garden cemetery, established in 1839, just after Laurel Hill (1836). Originally called Pere–Lachaise, after the first ever rural garden cemetery in Paris, it was renamed Monument Cemetery. The history of the cemetery is not well–publicized, but it grew to a fairly large size (28,000 graves despite its relatively small 15–acre spread). The last burial occurred in 1929, and by 1938, the cemetery had fallen into disrepair. By the 1950s, the land became more desirable that the cemetery itself, and Temple University, across the street, wanted to buy it and build a parking lot.

Monument Cemetery found itself waning, but Temple helped it to hasten down the wind. According to Tom Keels, neighbors wanted to keep the cemetery, but Temple held public hearings and convinced the city to condemn it and let the school purchase it. Supposedly the property was attracting teenagers who drank, then went out and committed crimes. The picture painted was that Monument Cemetery was an eyesore, and a blight on the neighborhood of North Philadelphia [duh, look at North Philly now – destroying that cemetery was supposed to prevent this?].

How was this allowed to happen? To put things into historical perspective, at this point in American history, people were not keen on Victoriana (anything from the era 1837–1901). Many Victorian era cemeteries fell into disrepair because people thought they were old fashioned. Lot owners in many cemeteries across the U.S. were actually embarrassed by the old–fashioned gaudiness of their own family plots and removed the decorative fencing and other ironwork to dispose of or sell for scrap. So even though many of Monument Cemetery's lot owners fought the eviction of their ancestors, there really was not much public outcry against plowing over the cemetery and building a parking lot and playground (as Temple and the City's Board of Education wanted). You can see a photograph of Monument Cemetery, c. 1950, at this link to the Temple University Libraries Archives:
http://digital.library.temple.edu/cdm/singleitem/collection/p245801coll0/id/5150/rec/2

So Temple got its wish in 1956. They removed the bodies (most of which were reburied in a mass grave at Lawnview Cemetery in Rockledge, a northeastern suburb of Philadelphia) and took most of the headstones, monuments, and other decorative stonework and dumped it all into the Delaware River. The tombstones were used as the foundation for the Betsy Ross Bridge. Today, some of them can still be seen at low tide. To get to them, you need to walk over the canal bridge on Hedley Street, approach the industrial site, and cut into the woods on the right side of the road. Your access is a break in the fence almost under Betsy herself. Close to the road this area is a dumping ground for old mattresses and sofas, further in it is partyland for transients. Walk the quarter mile path along the canal through the woods to the river.

**The Stones**

So we found the stones. I expected to see a few broken ones here and there poking out of the water, but was quite unprepared for the sight that presented itself. As we approached the river, we could plainly see gravestones scattered along the rocky shore. In fact, much of the rock that made up the shore itself was a mass of broken tombstones – some marble, but mostly elegantly carved and polished granite stones, coping from family plots, huge blocks of foundation granite used for large monuments. These apparently are the ones that tumbled off the dump trucks, rolling over the stones that had already been dumped. I realized this as we climbed down the ten–foot embankment, using tombstones for steps. They protruded out from the dirt, making you wonder just how many were there. Certainly more than were obvious.

River tides are a funny thing. I learned this from one of the fishermen I work with. I just assumed that all water bodies connected to an ocean had low tide in the morning and high tide at night. Turns out that most places have two high and two low tides each day, and the actual hour at which these occur depends upon the phases of the moon (so low tide times for a particular day, for instance, can be eight hours later on the same day a week later!). While tides are predictable, their timing was not very practical for my photographic purposes. Low tide was to occur at 1 p.m. on Good Friday during the month of April. Therefore, take a vacation day from work.

Good Friday was a perfect overcast day – flat lighting is good if you're not sure what the shooting conditions will be. As you can see from the chart excerpt at the beginning of this article, low tide occurred at this point in the Delaware River (tide times also change with your location!) at 12:57 pm. We arrived about 2 pm. The timing was fairly critical since (according to the chart above), by 6 pm the sea level would rise six feet above its lowest point (which was about where it was on our arrival), covering most of the stones we photographed. There was mud on many of the stones, indicating they were all underwater earlier that morning.

Leo and I walked along the shore maybe the length of a city block and counted about 50 whole stones, with an additional eight peeking out of the water. After 130 years, inscriptions are still clearly visible on them – granite doesn't fade as fast as people's memories.

Standing near the water, looking up at an embankment made primarily of tombstones, I felt like I was at the foot of Golgotha – this was Good Friday, after all. This was like beachcombing in Hell. Seeing piles of grave markers and monuments, shaded by trees hung with condoms and other trash, made me wonder how anyone could do this to a cemetery. Couldn't they at least bury the monuments, or smash them up into gravel? At the foot of the rubble was a headstone, which originally marked the grave of Capt. Babel H. Irons' wife, Mary (1823 – 1917). No sign of Irons' own marker, but what a great name! Every stone here has a story. After his death, it seems that Captain Irons had a 223–ton Philadelphia–based merchant sailing vessel named after him, so he must have been well–respected at the time.

According to the New York Times, a Marine Intelligence telegraph was received on Nov. 27, 1874 from the brig Castilian, which mentions Babel H. Irons. "...on the night of the 23d inst., in a south–east gale, lost boat, split foresail and jib, stove bulwarks, and had deck swept of galley, &c." The Irons stone here on the river shore stares at you like the final flare from a shipwreck.

Frequently, I'm asked me how a cemetery becomes 'abandoned.' There is probably a different reason for every abandoned cemetery. However, Monument Cemetery was not abandoned, let's be clear on that – it was destroyed. After reading what little is available on the Web about Monument Cemetery and after seeing the dumped stones, I had so many questions. I made an appointment to do some research at the Pennsylvania Historical Society in Philadelphia. In the next blog post, you can see what I dig up (pun intended).

# How Philadelphia's Monument Cemetery was Destroyed

Originally published Friday, May 6, 2011
https://thecemeterytraveler.blogspot.com/2011/05/how-monument-cemetery-was-destroyed.html

By the summer of 1956, the job of clearing Monument Cemetery was well under way. Bodies had already been removed from one section of the old grave yard. At that time, the University referring to it as PROGRESS, stated that "the old cemetery...will provide much needed parking space by fall."
–Things that Aren't There Anymore
(http://www.wrti.com/wrtifriend/things.html)

After my photo excursion to find the last remains of Philadelphia's

Monument Cemetery, I was overwhelmed with questions – my own as well as those posed by my readers. Hundreds of questions, literally, such as, how could some entity (Temple University, in this case) just buy a cemetery and build a parking lot over it? Was the cemetery actually abandoned? Supposedly, all the bodies were removed, but how did they do that? And the families were okay with it? When this happened in 1956, the cemetery was over a century old – did they contact the relatives of the 28,000 people buried there? Why were all the monuments and headstones dumped into the Delaware River? I get a weird feeling now whenever I drive over the Betsy Ross Bridge, like its somehow sacrilegious that granite tombstones are part of its foundation. (That's a photo of the bridge, at the beginning of this essay.)

They say the universe is finite, contained, and searchable, so, in an attempt to find answers, I paid a visit to the Pennsylvania Historical Society in Philadelphia. I knew from past visits here and to the Library Company of Philadelphia next door, that they had certain records related to area cemeteries. Once I got into the Historical Society to begin my research, I was amazed to find hundreds of bound volumes (handwritten as well as copied) of burial records and tombstone inscriptions from more cemeteries than I thought existed in the Philadelphia are, along with all their original deeds, charters, and annual reports. There were also vintage brochures and guidebooks (c. 1850) printed by the large Victorian garden cemeteries for advertising purposes. You can actually peruse these wonderful parchment–like and very fragile volumes from the Laurel Hill, Woodlands, and Mt. Vernon cemeteries in Philadelphia. Wonderful lithographs of monuments, chapels, and gatehouses adorn the pages, many of which either no longer exist or are so weather–worn as to be barely recognizable. It's obvious that such documentation is necessary for accurate restoration of cemetery sculpture and monuments (which people actually do, in case you were wondering). After about half an hour of searching, I came upon a three–volume set of documentation related to Monument Cemetery (which initially had been named Pere Lachaise, its namesake being the original Victorian garden cemetery in Paris opened in 1804).

In the set of burial records were tombstone inscriptions, an alphabetical listing of those interred, and legal documentation for the property. At the end of Volume One, there were dozens of copied newspaper clippings related to the battle to close the cemetery (mid–1950s). As I read through these clippings, certain things became clear – I better understood how a cemetery could be made to disappear.

In a nutshell, the cemetery had not been abandoned, it was destroyed. Bodies were reinterred elsewhere and most of the tombstones and monuments were dumped into the Delaware River, to be used as foundation rock for when the city built the Betsy Ross Bridge (connecting

Philadelphia to Camden, New Jersey). In my previous blog, "The Watery Remains of Monument Cemetery," I wrote about my excursion to find the stones, which are visible at low tide. Visible with a bit of work, that is. You can't just look down into the water and see them as you drive across the bridge. You can see them by boat, however, which I am sure is a startling sight to the unprepared.

*So that her high–born kinsmen came*
*And bore her away from me,*
*To shut her up in a sepulchre*
*In this kingdom by the sea.*
– from Annabel Lee, by Edgar Allan Poe

**How did Temple University acquire Monument Cemetery?**

As the universe expands, so do universities. In the 1950s, Temple was developing itself into a commuter school, and needed more parking – and those fifteen acres across the street were just being wasted on a cemetery. They'd actually been trying to acquire the cemetery since 1928, but continually met with resistance from the cemetery's owners.

According to records, the owners of Monument Cemetery only had about $11,000 in assets by 1953. This was barely enough income for the owners to provide necessary maintenance to the buildings and upkeep to the graves. With no new burials since 1929, there had been no income for 24 years (there was no available burial space left). The cemetery had been in business for 114 years, and its fifteen acres were filled to capacity with 28,000 graves. As a result, the cemetery physically deteriorated to the point where it invited vandalism. The owners were actively trying to sell it, but were incensed at potential buyers' (including Temple) plans for the land. Eventually Temple lobbied the city government to condemn it, and ended up acquiring it after that occurred. According to the Philadelphia Evening Bulletin of May 28, 1953, public hearings were held in which a number of people testified that the cemetery was a haven for rats, criminals, tramps, and sex offenders.

It appears that legal title passed from the owners of Monument Cemetery to the City of Philadelphia, but I could find no record of the amount the owners were compensated. Once a government determines that private property is needed for the completion of a public project (Temple is a public, i.e. state school), the owners will likely lose their property. The property owner is entitled to fair compensation for the loss, but it appears that Monument's owners received far less (if anything). Kind of like when my grandmother's house was taken through "eminent domain" by a local municipality so that a playground could be built.

Estimated value of the land in the part of Philadelphia in which Monument Cemetery was situated was about $40,000 per acre, making the cemetery's fifteen acres worth about $600,000. Temple had previously stated that it could not afford to buy the land at that price. As Lawnview Cemetery (in Rockledge, a Philadelphia suburb) was later awarded a $700,000 contract by the city for the transfer and perpetual care of the bodies, I find it hard to believe the city paid Monument's owners anything for the land. The nearly bankrupt cemetery was railroaded into oblivion.

**Did they actually remove the bodies?**

Well, if you can believe the newspapers, yes. But who knows? There was a photograph published by the Philadelphia Evening Bulletin of the demolition showing a crane hoisting a concrete crypt out of the ground. But what of the thousands of older burials that only had wooden coffins, coffins that had partially or totally decomposed? I began to wonder what sort of notifications were sent to families whose loved ones were buried there … eviction notices? Did they board up the periphery of the cemetery so people couldn't see the coffins coming out of the ground? Did people care? I had to find out, and I hoped the Historical Society would provide.

The dozens of newspaper clippings mentioned above cover the final two years of the cemetery's existence – from 1954 (when its fate was mired in political intrigue) to 1956 (when the cemetery was condemned, given to Temple, and dug up). During the time that the cemetery's owners were trying to sell it in above–board fashion, Temple had made low offers, and was turned down. In its relentless quest for the land, Temple resorted to political tactics to have the ground condemned, while maintaining an air of empathy by declaring that if it acquired the cemetery, it would also have to dig up Temple's founder, Dr. Russell Conwell, and his wife, who were buried there. In the end, they moved those graves across the street near Conwell Hall (where I used to go to pay my daughter's tuition).

**How were lot holders notified?**

Apparently, the majority were not. But first, let's do some math. In 1954 when the cemetery owners sent out mailings to lot holders announcing the likelihood that graves would have to be moved when the cemetery was sold, they only had reliable contact information for 748 families – out of 28,000 burials. Of these 748, only 400 lot holders responded to mailings – 300 of whom met to vote on which cemetery they would want their ancestors moved to. Two cemeteries bid on the contract – Lawnview Cemetery and Philadelphia Memorial Park in Frazer, PA. Lawnview was chosen after a nine–month debate, mainly because it was closer to Monument Cemetery (more convenient for the lot holders) and it would charge less for removal of the bodies.

So only 300 family plots were moved to Lawnview along with their monuments and headstones (though you would be hard pressed to locate more than a few grave markers in the vast field where the bodies now lay). I would assume that some of the remaining 100 of the contacted lot holders had their loved ones moved privately to different cemeteries at their own expense. But the vast majority of the 28,000 bodies, it seems, went unclaimed!

In order to clear the land of human remains and stonework, 28,000 bodies had to be re–located, about 20,000 of which were unclaimed. These 20,000 – a staggering number – were the ones that were quietly dumped into a large mass grave at Lawnview Cemetery. Their monuments and any of the elaborately carved stonework that hadn't been claimed by relatives were sold to developers, and hauled to the Philadelphia shore of the Delaware River to be used as part of the foundation to build the Betsy Ross Bridge (construction was completed in 1976). Monuments, including major works of art by 19th century sculptors, were dumped into the river to be used as "riprap" (granite or concrete rubble from building and paving demolition commonly used to protect shorelines from water or ice erosion).

Oddly, the original stone walls of Monument Cemetery remain. They border the Temple University athletic field, directly across Broad Street from Temple's Conwell Hall. Why they were left, puzzles me. The holes in the top of the wall can be clearly seen, where iron fence posts that were inserted and fastened with lead beading. The front wall is parallel to Broad Street, while the side walls extend west to the next city block. There has been discussion since 2015 about Temple digging this up to build a new football field. My guess is they don't want to dig too deep, as no doubt bodies will be found.

**Forgotten graves? Not totally.**

What of the people whose loved ones were buried at Monument, were they unaware of its closing? Many of my Cemetery Traveler blog readers are appalled by what happened to this cemetery, shocked by the callousness of a modern society. Looking back, it seems that it all occurred precisely because of the modernism of our society and how we value "progress." It all sounds like Temple and the City of Philadelphia tied up Monument Cemetery in a neat little package which made a handful of people happy. Today, it's a different story, as I come upon these chilling comments on my blog related to Monument Cemetery:

*"I am overwhelmed with sorrow. I just found out that my great grandfather* was buried

*in Monument in 1898. I confirmed he is in the "common grave" in Lawnview. Finding out about the stones in the river, and the seemingly slip shod manner of trying to find owners/relatives of the deceased makes me think twice about my final resting place. Hopefully, we will all pass on the respect due the deceased and not forget their final resting place. What a wrenching story this was. Thanks for all your research."* – Sally G.

*"I was a Temple student when bodies, aka remains, were removed from Monument. Even then, Temple was a commuting school. It was private, not a state university. Not all gravestones were removed. I remember marble ones being smashed to pieces by workers with sledge hammers. I also remember wooden coffins being opened by workers with hooks. The high water table had flooded these coffins and what remained of the bodies were extracted. I assume the wooden coffins, or what's left of them, remain underground to this day."* – Bill B.

*"They didn't move all those bodies. Anybody who understands how construction and refuse industries operate (hint– Mafia) knows they didn't bother with detail. Or at least for me it's a gut wrenching, all knowing feeling of what really occurred here. The desecration of the graves and grave markers – not to mention Temple University and the City's behavior – it's all nothing short of astounding. My condolences to the descendants who have the misfortune of finding out about this. And I suppose those descendants who never learn of this are just plain lucky."* – Anon.

*"Thank you for sharing this story, one that needs to be told and shared."* – Rick G.

## Physical Evidence of Humanity's Callousness

As I mentioned in my previous blog posting, "The Watery Remains of Monument Cemetery," my friend Leo and I trekked out to the Delaware river and found the site of the discarded tombstones from Monument Cemetery. We only actually found about 50 exposed whole grave markers, so the rest must must be either buried, drowned, or reduced to rubble. When you think about it, roughly twenty thousand bodies were unclaimed, so several thousand gravemarkers must have been discarded.

Supposedly, John Sartain's Egyptian–style monument was dumped into the Delaware and is now part of the Betsy Ross Bridge. Sartain was one of the original designers of Monument Cemetery; he and his family were buried there. Sartain's is not a name with which many are familiar, but to whom the literary world owes a debt of gratitude. He was Edgar Allen Poe's friend, colleague, and publisher while Poe lived in Philadelphia.

John Sartain was a true renaissance man – publisher, engraver, artist, and architect. He was responsible for the design of Monument Cemetery's gatehouse and the cemetery's immense (over 70 feet high) central monument to George Washington and General Lafayette.

Link to photo of gatehouse:
https://digital.librarycompany.org/islandora/object/digitool%3A99136?solr_nav%5Bid%5D=7c6892d2f6ddf2d0e5ed&solr_nav%5Bpage%5D=0&solr_nav%5Boffset%5D=12

Link to photo of the dismantling of Washington and Lafayette monument:
http://digital.library.temple.edu/cdm/singleitem/collection/p15037coll3/id/479/rec/4

According to Sartain's autobiography, The Reminiscences of a Very Old Man (D. Appleton and Company, 1899), "Monument Cemetery" derived its name from this monument. Sartain's own memorial lives with the fishes – supposedly dumped as unceremoniously as the rest of the stones.

Sartain's Union Magazine featured the first publication of Poe's haunting poem, "Annabel Lee," which is about a rivalry that resulted in a watery death. Appropos of the cemetery's own struggle with its foes, which ended with one of the parties suffering a watery demise.

*And this was the reason that, long ago,*
*In this kingdom by the sea, …*
*So that her high–born kinsmen came*
*And bore her away from me,*
*To shut her up in a sepulchre*
*In this kingdom by the sea.*

– from Annabel Lee, by Edgar Allan Poe

# Pit Bulls, Deer Ticks, and Poison Ivy

Originally published Wednesday, September 1, 2010
https://thecemeterytraveler.blogspot.com/2010/09/pit-bulls-deer-ticks-and-poison-ivy.html

Last weekend (August 28, 2010), my friend Frank and I explored Mount Moriah Cemetery (est. 1855) in West Philadelphia. Though I'd been there innumerable times, it's been years since I'd explored the central monument area, which is way overgrown with trees, cascading picker vines, and poison ivy. Essentially, it's a forest, only with tombstones in it!

Frank had heard stories about the cemetery being wild and untamed. He asked me if he should bring a weapon. A weapon? Well maybe boots and long pants (even in this heat) because of the deer ticks. Truth be told, Mount Moriah is in a dilapidated, economically challenged section of town (where all the best cemeteries usually are), and I agreed we should at least bring baseball bats. However, he was referring to the "family of wild pit bulls" he heard lived in the cemetery! I had my doubts.

I figured if there was a family of pit bulls, they'd be living in some shelter, e.g. the crumbling brownstone gatehouse. So we decided that should be our first stop. Upon arriving, we explored but only found sordid bedding littered with condom wrappers, and ... piles of tombstones. Tombstones? Some from the late 1800s, some from 2006. Why? In looking at Mount Moriah's website (a private site, unassociated with the cemetery itself, which existed as of 2010, but was taken down around 2011) it appears that stones get moved and disappear. A genealogist's nightmare. They also say on the site, if you're planning to visit the cemetery, "It may be worth a trip, but be prepared for confusion, frustration and disappointment." Hmmm. Now that's enticing.

Mount Moriah's wildness harbored criminal activity of many sorts – a great place for johns to drive and park with prostitutes, and for stolen cars to be torched. Half a dozen years prior to our visit, I was exploring this same area with a friend and was amazed to come upon a large, clearly cultivated marijuana patch. In the middle of one heavily weeded section (pun intended), there was a clearing about twenty by twenty feet, and in the center were rows of mature pot plants. We did have the good sense to remove ourselves from the area rather quickly. There was no trace of the crop on my current visit.

We actually found some interesting things in the open and trimmed newer section of the cemetery (on Kingsessing Ave.), like a marble monument to a U.S. Naval officer who was associated with the Monitor, the Civil War submarine that engaged the Merrimac in the famous battle of the ironclads. The eight–foot–long marble sculpture is actually shaped like the Monitor! Quite a find, certainly not disappointing. We also peeked into the chained–up mausoleum nearby and were surprised to see a shattered marble crypt door allowing a rare voyeuristic view of the 100–year–old wooden casket inside.

Frank and I decided to drive my car as far as we could into the main section of the cemetery, where the tops of very elaborate, expensive, and grafittied monuments peeked over the tops of trees. Some of the original weed–covered roads are still used by people to deliver old sofas and tires to their final resting place, so they are somewhat drivable (a jeep would be your vehicle of choice here). The gigantic monument in the center of the forest, commemorates an 1862 Masonic "Grand Tyler." Its column must be

40 feet high and 6 feet thick at the base, topped with the largest marble compass I've ever seen. After hacking our way to the base of it, Frank astutely pointed out that I was standing knee–deep in poison ivy! We made our way out of the thicket and back to the car. In one area thick with flesh–ripping thorned vines, I bent down to duck under and some critter darted away from me through the underbrush.

Back to the car—driving through this jungle, straddling washed–out craters in the road and avoiding being whipped in the face by tree branches was like being on one of those Disney jungle rides at Universal Studios—you half expect a velociraptor to poke its head out of the thicket! Which is about when we saw the pit bulls…

Two large brown puppies went scampering off down a path near the tall monument. We had stopped here earlier to photograph it, but hadn't noticed the dogs—of course we were looking up at the time …. Gee, let's get out now and see how protective the mother is…! No really, at that point, I wished the convertible top of my car went up a bit faster. At that point we mutually agreed that is was time to bravely drive away.

At one point on a side road, or path, really, we dead–ended at a pile of lumber, busted up sofas, and other rubbish. As I backed the car out for about ten minutes to get to a different side–road so we could turn around without getting lost, it became apparent to me that Saabs are just not good off–road vehicles. Well, the Mount Moriah website did say to be prepared for confusion and frustration.... With a sigh of relief, we found our way out of the woods into a clearing, and then back to familiar territory— the pile of unused concrete crypts near the old crumbling 1855 brownstone gatehouse. We were certainly not disappointed that the mama pit bull decided to keep a low profile that day.

Is Mount Moriah a sad commentary on our city or a wondrous attraction for the urban explorer of abandoned places? I can't be judgmental as to the former and am sorry that the cemetery has been allowed to devolve to this sad state. However, it allows one to contemplate the detritus of human endeavor. We erect monuments to the deceased (often ourselves) for a purpose, but attempts to preserve memories can sometimes be undermined. Vandals, time, and weather erode efforts at immortality and the corruption of the cemetery seems to affirm, rather than deny the decay down below. Seeing it in this condition, you feel you are witnessing the final disappearance of the spirits of the dead.

**Author's note:**

I wrote the above account in 2010, never guessing that years later I would find myself on the Board of Directors of a Friends group making every attempt to save this massive historic cemetery. How it got to the condition I described in 2010 seems to have been a result of gross mismanagement and negligence—perhaps 100 years of this. When Harry Houdini visited the grave of his idol Robert Heller here in 1910, he was dismayed at the condition of the cemetery. But it doesn't have to be that way. If people join together for a common goal, miracles sometimes happen. Respect for the dead is a powerful thing.

This was the first of several early blogs I posted about my experiences at Mount Moriah. They got quite a few people riled up. Local residents, descendants of the interred, the City of Philadelphia, and numerous other concerned citizens nationwide were appalled and irate. The situation at the cemetery got to the point where the City of Philadelphia felt obligated to step in and haul away the abandoned cars, round up the feral dogs, and barricade the entrances. A grassroots Friends group stepped up: The Friends of Mount Moriah Cemetery. After a few run–ins with them, they became convinced, as did I, that I wanted to help save the cemetery. At approximately 300 acres and over 80,000 graves, Mount Moriah is the largest cemetery in Pennsylvania. It likely was the largest abandoned cemetery in the U.S. in 2010.

In those early days, having no knowledge is sometimes exactly what is needed to find a solution, and I certainly qualified. I could fill volumes with what I didn't know about cemetery restoration. Sometimes you just need to destroy something in order to create anew. Mount Moriah is no longer abandoned. The Friends of Mount Moriah Cemetery, Inc. has worked tirelessly since 2012, engaging thousands of volunteers to clean up and take back from nature this overgrown green space in urban Philadelphia. If not for the efforts of so many concerned, Mount Moriah would have been left to die on the vine — or by the vine, more literally. Such a dramatic display of volunteerism is hardly revolutionary (although Betsy Ross is in fact buried here); however, the sustained effort certainly is.

# The Rescue of Mount Moriah Cemetery

Originally published Tuesday, September 23, 2014
https://thecemeterytraveler.blogspot.com/2014/09/the-rescue-of-mount-moriah-cemetery.html

Those of you who follow my Cemetery Traveler blog already know that Mount Moriah Cemetery is near and dear to my heart. I had been exploring this overgrown, neglected Victorian cemetery since the late 1990s. By 2011, it was officially abandoned by its owners and left to grow wild. According to anecdotal reports, the cemetery began to deteriorate on a grand scale in the 1970s.

It is so large (approximately 300 acres), it spans two counties – Philadelphia and Delaware. Around 2011, I began noticing small groups of people there when I would visit, cutting weeds and picking up trash. I would be lugging my camera gear with me, documenting the deplorable conditions and writing about it on The Cemetery Traveler.

I'd like to think those early blogs altered peoples' mindset about this property, and brought about public awareness of its condition. Certainly, people were incensed. They demanded that the City of Philadelphia do something about it, yet the city did not own the property. Something needed to be done, and only one small group of people had the answer. Historic preservation of a cemetery is all about respect, respect for those who came before us, respect for ourselves. We need to preserve the past;

people need tangible links to their past.

After a few chance meetings with these weed cutters and trash picker–uppers at Mount Moriah, I introduced myself. I was curious as to what they were up to. Most people I'd seen in the vast jungles of this cemetery up to that point were up to no good. This was different.

They were wary of me due to the several blogs I had posted based on my experiences there. They took personal offense. This was a group of volunteers calling themselves The Friends of Mount Moriah Cemetery, and they were here to save it. The planned to secure it, clean it up, take it back from Nature – whose tall trees and weeds had covered ninety percent of the grounds. These people were hacking through the undergrowth with machetes. My kind of people. Its one thing to be a voyeuristic urban explorer, but totally another to work toward correcting the ills of mankind.

Before long, I volunteered to be part of the Friends group. With some trepidation, I am sure, they let me in. I worked on multimedia outreach, websites, newsletters, and the like. Before long, I found myself on the all–volunteer Board of Directors of The Friends of Mount Moriah Cemetery, Inc., working to bring it back from ruin. The blog post below documents a major step in the stabilization, preservation, and future of this historic property. You'll read quite a bit about abandoned cemeteries on my blog. Most are not lucky enough to have an outcome as positive as Mount Moriah's.

**The Rescue of Mount Moriah Cemetery**

September 17, 2014 was a landmark day for Mount Moriah Cemetery (which resides partially in Philadelphia, and partially in Yeadon, Pennsylvania). In Philadelphia City Hall, Room 416, Honorable Judge John W. Herron heard the petition by the newly–formed Mount Moriah Cemetery Preservation Corporation to dissolve the Articles of the legacy (1855) Mount Moriah Cemetery Association and name the newly–formed (2012) corporation as the receiver. After hearing an hour's worth of testimony and reviewing the documentation, he gave his approval.

What does this mean? "Receivership," by legal definition, refers to a "court order whereby all the property subject to dispute in a legal action is placed under the dominion and control of an independent person known as a receiver." In this action, Judge Herron dissolved the 159–year–old Mount Moriah Cemetery Association, whose last officer died in 2004. The Mount Moriah Cemetery Preservation Corporation now has legal custodial responsibility for the property, including its tangible and intangible assets and rights, since the original company could not meet its obligations.

From the Friends of Mount Moriah Cemetery, Inc. website: http://friendsofmountmoriahcemetery.org/about/recent–history/

*"In December of 2012, Yeadon Borough and Philadelphia established the Mount Moriah Cemetery Preservation Corporation. This not–for–profit organization will likely become the Receiver of the property whereby it will be authorized to act on behalf of the Court for the Mount Moriah Cemetery Association in specified areas of business operations. Because of the complexity of the issues and in order to insure a similar situation does not occur in the future, ongoing municipal involvement is important. While the organization would be led by the municipal governments, the organization's board is diverse in experience and ethnicity."*

For this overgrown several–hundred–acre cemetery that was abandoned in 2011, the appointment of a receiver for the property means that now there will be a legal entity to begin the process of operating the cemetery, conducting business, and winding up the affairs of the old Mount Moriah Cemetery Association. It also means, and is hoped, that Mount Moriah can once again become an active cemetery, meeting the needs of several racial, religious and socioeconomic stakeholders. Mount Moriah is one of the few cemeteries in the Philadelphia area known to accept Muslim burials and is one of two in the vicinity known to accept communal burials – burials where three bodies share one grave and are a less expensive option for many families.

The appointment of the receiver does not affect the rights of anyone who has a contract to be buried in Mount Moriah – it actually makes it more likely that this can legally be accomplished in the near future. While the cemetery was closed, burials could not legally take place. The new non–profit organization is dedicated to securing the future of the Mount Moriah Cemetery. With its a seven–member board, it will assume responsibility and report to the court twice a year on its progress in restoring the grounds and improving business operations.

The receivership hearing barely lasted an hour. On hand were members of The Friends of Mount Moriah Cemetery, Inc. (FOMMCI) Board of Directors (myself included), members of the Board of Directors of the new Mount Moriah Cemetery Preservation Corporation, and legal representation by Matthew N. McClure and other attorneys at Ballard Spahr L.L.P. As part of the attorneys' prepared argument as to why the receivership should be granted (with the goal that Mount Moriah would be saved from further deterioration), Mr. McClure stated that the cemetery has 5,000 veterans, including 23 recipients of the Congressional Medal of Honor. In response, Judge Herron made the pointed comment that all those buried at Mount Moriah deserve sanctity and respect, whether they have medals or not.

From about the time it was abandoned in March of 2011, until the September 17, 2014 hearing, the cemetery has been maintained primarily through volunteer efforts organized by the Friends of Mount Moriah

Cemetery, Inc., a 501(c)3 non–profit organization, with assistance from the City of Philadelphia and Yeadon Borough. Since 2011, the Friends have organized events with thousands of volunteers who have participated in cleanups, restoration, grave location, genealogical research, and historic tours. This will likely continue into the new era. Major fund–raising efforts will now be underway to make more significant improvements, for instance in the areas of security and infrastructure.

Brian Abernathy, president of the new organization, (and then executive director of the Philadelphia Redevelopment Authority) was one of the witnesses called to testify at the hearing, basically to ensure that the City of Philadelphia would play a managing role in the continued operation of Mount Moriah. Other witnesses (all of whom occupy Board positions with the Mount Moriah Cemetery Preservation Corporation) were Yeadon Borough mayor Rohan Hepkins, Nevin Mann (president of the Pennsylvania Cemetery Association and resident expert in the death care industry), and Paulette Rhone. Paulette, whose husband is buried at Mount Moriah, is president of the FOMMCI.

Yeadon Borough is now expected to take a greater role in preservation of that portion of Mount Moriah that resides within its borders. Mayor Hepkins stated that Mount Moriah Cemetery is a vital part of Yeadon and contributes to the quality of life in the community.

Several members of the FOMMCI were present at the hearing in addition to Paulette Rhone: Ed Snyder, vice president Bill Warwick, Treasurer Ken Smith, and Secretary Sue Facciolli. All were overjoyed at the outcome. It felt like a successful culmination of three years of hard work. Yet this is just the beginning of a new era in Mount Moriah's existence.

Brian Abernathy, President of the Mount Moriah Cemetery Preservation Corporation, in a 2015 letter to stakeholders, summed up the cemetery's recent past and alluded to its future. He stated that over the last several years, the cemetery had been greatly improved due to the efforts of the Friends of Mount Moriah Cemetery, Inc., the volunteer organization that was formed to steward the cemetery after it was abandoned in 2011. The Friends organization will continue to exist, working in conjunction with the newly–formed corporation. In addition to keeping up the physical appearance of the cemetery and performing genealogical research, efforts will expand in the areas of security, maintenance, and determining a strategic direction for the long–term viability of the property. (http://friendsofmountmoriahcemetery.org/wp–content/uploads/2015/11/Stakeholder–Update.pdf)

My wife said to me around 2015, "If you clean up the cemetery, what will you take pictures of?" In 2015, only about thirty percent of Mount Moriah's massive area had been cut back. Most was still dense forest. I told her it would be years before I ran out of things to photograph there. And during that future period, I would learn more about myself, local history, architecture, death, and respecting those who came before us.

# SECTION 3:

# SEX AND DEATH

You were waiting for this, weren't you? I mean, how could I write about death without also writing about sex? Whatever could sex and cemeteries have in common, you ask? Turns out sex and death are very closely related in our psyches. We seem to be simultaneously death phobic and sexually driven – death and desire seem to conjugate in some fashion in our minds, a philosophy of opposites. But do they conjugate in our cemeteries? That is, does live sex (I mean, between people) occur in our memory gardens, creating memories besides the ones originally intended? Sure it does. I've heard about it, I've seen it, I've done it.

*"OMG....I can't believe what I'm reading. But to be honest....uh, I've had some amorous trysts in the back of some mausoleums myself. Been a long while but memorable."* – Robert G.

# Sex and Death

Originally published SUNDAY, APRIL 27, 2014
https://thecemeterytraveler.blogspot.com/2014/04/cemetery–lovers–sex–and–death.html

Sex and death. Eros and Thanatos. Sigmund Freud believed them to be our inner drives, forces that both coincide and conflict. As humans we seem to be simultaneously sexually driven and death phobic.

The sculpture in the photograph above is a copy of Psyche Revived by Love's Kiss (think Cupid and Psyche), by the Venetian sculptor Antonio

Canova [1757 – 1822]. The original resides in the Louvre. The one I photographed is in the Hollywood Forever Cemetery in Hollywood, California. Cheesy, yes, but I actually prefer the knock–off to the original! The cemetery is cleverly described by its owners as the final resting place of Hollywood's immortals, which includes, quite appropriately, Rudolph Valentino. My photograph of this statue so epitomizes love, that I was asked if I would allow it to grace the cover of the February 2013 issue of The Journal of the Center for Freudian Analysis and Research (Issue No.23 "On Love," February 2013), published in Britain.

Cupid, or Eros, is waking his love, Psyche, with a kiss. [In Roman mythology, Cupid (Latin Cupido, for "desire") is the god of desire, affection, and erotic love. The sculpture epitomizes not only love, but death as well. Freud theorized that human nature is grounded in two basic instincts: Eros and Thanatos, the libido and mortido – the life instinct and death instinct.

So, then, if Cupid, or Eros, with his erotic embrace, is reviving the woman with a kiss, is she dead? Is Antonio Canova's sculpture as much about death as it appears to be about love? The meaning behind the statue lies in Greek mythology, not far from Walt Disney's Sleeping Beauty. It is an allegory about love overcoming death. As a piece of sculpture in a cemetery, it can easily symbolize life after death – immortality.

But let's return to sex. While teenagers may use our cemeteries as trysting places because it's the only place they can find privacy, adults do it for many other reasons. Its exciting, its forbidden (sort of, I guess, though I've never actually seen any signs posted … ), and it is the closest many of us will get to experiencing human nature's two basic instincts at the same time: Eros and Thanatos. Sure there's autoerotic asphyxia (strangulation during sex), but that's going off the deep end. Most people don't need to go to such extremes to get off. Freud theorized that Thanatos, the instinct of death, or aggression, drives us as strongly as does Eros, our instinct for life. Eros drives us toward attraction and reproduction while Thanatos drives us to our destruction.

If you accept this, it explains why so much of our entertainment (movies, books, and television) keeps us riveted with a teetering balance of sex and death. We enjoy this, for the most part. Sometimes, real life mimics fiction. Take for instance the couple I witnessed who showed up at the cemetery for my "night photography" event – without cameras. As the group headed off into the cemetery with the instructors, the couple disappeared in the opposite direction. (Do I need to draw you a picture?) While such things may not be expressly forbidden, it is usually easier to get forgiveness than permission!

Doing it in a cemetery must be titillating to a certain subset of the population. I've stumbled upon skindiving couples a few times, but I can't imagine that hordes of people WANT to do this. Sometimes, though, I understand that business may necessitate it. Take for instance the prostitute who recently approached several cemetery grounds keepers (separately, but on the same day) while in the course of their duties. This was her line: "Are you single? Because I don't want any wives involved in this. My apartment has ghosts. Can you come and check it out for me?" After her third attempt failed, she left.

I myself have been propositioned by prostitutes – twice – while photographing inside cemeteries! So while some of my research depends on secondary sources, my primary research corroborates the data. I am happy to say my actual sexual encounters in graveyards did not involve prostitutes. And I was between marriages, for the record. I realize that prostitution in graveyards is strictly business – the parties are not looking for thrills, its just cheaper than getting a room. Its also less embarrassing than having the desk clerk offer you the hourly rate as you check in ....

So, maybe cemeteries should have "No Soliciting" signs on their gates? Or "No Engaging" signs .... I know of a cemetery where men (whom I did *not* know!) have driven onto the grounds with prostitutes in their cars, found a secluded spot and done the deed. You may think I'm going for the full Pinocchio on this topic but its true – I've seen it many times. I've unfortunately and accidentally, driven by such scenes. Several times. A friend of mine who volunteers at a cemetery saw a taxi parked on the grounds recently, so she approached it, and then noticed that it was bouncing up and down! Two people were on the back seat while the DRIVER sat patiently behind the steering wheel! (No doubt the meter was ticking away.)

And then there was the story I was told about the two volunteers taking a break from their tree-cutting in an overgrown cemetery that shall not be named. A pickup truck came driving into the densely forested area in which they were working. Thinking it was just another volunteer, they went about their business, picked up their chainsaws, and started them up. The scene that resulted took them quite by surprise. The pickup truck driver, a male, who had a woman next to him, had quickly thrown the truck in reverse and was flooring it to get away from the madmen with the chainsaws! The truck was sliding in the dirt, hitting trees, and breaking branches as the driver, no doubt in a royal panic, tried to get out of there. Serves you right, buddy.

But getting back to the business at hand, let us return to Eros versus Thanatos as they relate to the thrill of sex in a cemetery. Personally, I was too scared of being caught to be, shall we say, effective? Years ago, a partner and I were actually arrested in a similar situation, having to pay a fine only for trespassing – the police dropped the indecent exposure charge as there were no witnesses other than the cop who caught (and was no doubt watching) us. So while I've left my wild ways behind me, others obviously find the inherent danger of sex in cemeteries to be very stimulating. Not only due to the chance of being caught, I suppose, but also because of the very real possibility of being eaten by zombies.

Many of us are as obsessed with death as we are with sex, but less openly. We fear death, though it fascinates us. These inner drives, as Freud says, both coincide and conflict. So the life force in us is as strong as the death force, and while the drives may not be equal in everyone, they are certainly present, and often intermingle. This was never so prevalent as it was in the Victorian era, when artists had seemingly free reign to sculpt nude or partially nude statues for use as cemetery monuments. While the sculptures aren't exactly arousing, sexually, they are indeed suggestive. Perhaps their intent was to get our minds off dismal death, and to think instead about life and its beauty, as well as the joys of reproduction.

So can nude cemetery photography be much different? I don't mean photographing nude statues, but the photographing of nude humans in graveyards. It happens. On occasion, I've seen exhibits of such work, though you'd be hard–pressed to find any examples of it were you to actually search the Internet. It's a rather taboo subject, for all the reasons you can possibly imagine. There's that whole respect thing. I've never done this myself, but then who would want to see photos of me naked in a cemetery?

I know a fellow who works at a cemetery and he occasionally sees a clandestine nude photo shoot here and there. He politely asks the photographer and model to pack up and leave, as it may upset other visitors who may be visiting for other reasons. In one instance, he chased a vehicle from spot to spot over the course of a day as a woman dressed only in a cape would throw it over herself, jump into the passenger side of the vehicle and the driver would speed off. Sounds totally disrespectful, but can these artists be that much different from the Victorian–era sculptors who created the sensual, half–nude mourning art statues in the first place?

The fear of death fascinates us, but we avoid it like, well, the plague. Can the act of having sex in a cemetery somehow privately, subconsciously, help us come to terms with our own mortality? Does getting boned in the boneyard put a more enjoyable face on death, making part of it a pleasurable experience? Think back on those sensual cemetery statues, they're more life–affirming than death–centric, aren't they? Sex in a cemetery, then, may reinforce in us a feeling of life, which really was the original intent of the architects of the early garden cemeteries. Victorians believed if death is portrayed as beautiful, perhaps it will lose its sting. What's more beautiful than sex?

That said, if you've ever actually tried to have cemetery sex, you might have noticed that the environs can produce a certain, well, frisson of discomfort. Pleasurable to some, but downright distracting to others, making certain things, well, kind of ... difficult. If you try it, you're sure to see that its not as easy as you might think, from the physical or mental perspective! You can, however, look forward to basking in the afterglow as you pick deer ticks off your naked bodies ….

# The Art of Sensual Statues in Cemeteries

Originally published Monday, February 14, 2011
https://thecemeterytraveler.blogspot.com/2011/02/art–of–sensual–statues–in–cemeteries.html

On walking through just about any Victorian cemetery established after 1850, one is likely to see sensual female figures, carved from a variety of material – granite, marble, bronze. This is especially true in France, the birthplace of the "garden cemetery." For the uninitiated, garden cemeteries are essentially outdoor sculpture gardens, conceived in Europe in the Victorian era (1837 – 1901) to try and dispel some of the fear and bleakness associated with death and dying. Pere Lachaise in Paris and in Highgate in London are examples, though we find a great deal more sensual sculptures in France and Italy than we do in England.

The practice carried across the Pond in 1831 with the founding of Mount Auburn Cemetery (Cambridge, MA) and then Laurel Hill in 1836 (Philadelphia, PA). Statues in these and other Victorian cemeteries hearken back to a time when these unique memorial gardens served the public as a pleasant getaway from the noisy city. Now forgotten by the public and worn by the elements, this rare artwork was enjoyed by our ancestors long before museums, galleries, and parks came into being.

Now, you'd think statues of semi–nude women would have clashed with staunch Victorian sensibilities, wouldn't you? Especially in a cemetery – a reverent and respectful place frequented by the public! What role do these women play in the grieving process? They are symbolic, of course, but of what (besides affluence)? These typically life–sized sensual figures do give memorial parks a feeling of life, which really was the intent of the architects of early garden cemeteries.

In his book, Death: The Trip of a Lifetime (Harper Collins, 1993), Greg Palmer offers that in many cultures, women are the designated grievers. Ok, but why physically attractive females? David Robinson notes in his book Saving Graces (W. W. Norton, 1995), that their gowns are revealing and they are often topless or nude. He goes on to say that these statues were usually individually commissioned and sculpted, often by famous sculptors. In Western artistic tradition, the ability to accurately depict the female figure is what most defines artistic talent. So again, why physically attractive females? While their countenance may effectively express true sorrow and loss (even anguish), there are no ugly angels.

Besides the fact that most professional sculptors were male (we'll assume at least some of them, like Rodin, were heterosexual) and these commissions afforded them a regular income, sensual statues provided an opportunity for them to bring their artistic fantasies to life for a noble purpose. A female friend of mine once referred to such sensual mourning statuary as "Mourn Porn."

## Whose is Bigger?

So that covers females, but what about the male nude? Why do we see no copies of Michaelangelo's (anatomically correct) David in cemeteries? Maybe because the results would generate such public outcry, that the penises would be broken off, as was done to the Oscar Wilde monument in Paris' Pere Lachaise Cemetery! (Afterwards, the cemetery's director supposedly used it as a paperweight.)

While its true that we see a male angel once in a great while, most male statues in cemeteries depict the actual deceased man, often in a formal or noble pose. The allusion to male sexuality in mourning art is a bit more subtle, usually. Maybe you have to view it from a female perspective, but don't all those tall obelisks below seem a bit phallocentric? In fact the tallest funeral monument in the United States was erected (pun intended) in Philadelphia's Woodlands Cemetery in 1897, an obelisk that stands 150 feet high!

It seems that when male sexuality is involved, the results get pretty dramatic. There was an incident in a Philadelphia suburb in 2003 that blatantly brought to light the competitive nature between two men. Rival businessmen Goodin (1836–1890) and Gallagher (1834–1915) were both buried in the St. Denis Church Cemetery in Havertown, PA. Goodin died at age 54, leaving orders to erect an imposing 20–foot–tall monolith atop a 10–foot–tall granite base (we do like to call attention to ourselves!). Missing his friend and favorite adversary, Gallagher slyly bought the neighboring grave plot. He would wait 25 years before death let him claim final victory: an even more magnificent monolith of paler granite set atop an ornate base, the whole structure soaring to a pyramidal point about three feet higher than Goodin's highest point. In 2003, a storm toppled both monoliths. I suppose this is typical of men getting their brains caught in their zipper.

So let's try to put all this Mourn Porn in perspective. If death is portrayed as beautiful, perhaps it will lose its sting. For Romeo and Juliet, as with the Romantic era in general (1825 – 1900), death was the focus of extreme emotion and the ultimate expression of love (Robinson, 1995). This period of time coincides with Victorian era, in which the idea of death in art and popular culture became less associated with horror and fright and more with love and desire. No other era in Western culture has ever exhibited to such an extent the artistic emphasis on death as a visible part of the consciousness of an entire population.

In her book Mourning Art and Jewelry (Schiffer, 2004), Maureen DeLorme tells us that the pressures of continually facing death as an intrusion (French Revolution, Napoleanic Wars, high mortality from plagues and disease, etc.) made the need to keep both the presence of the departed near at hand while at the same time bidding farewell. So the idea of sculpted sensual beings in cemeteries became a tangible realization of a new Western psychology. Their purpose? To comfort the living and soften the finality of death. While angels may epitomize the tension between freedom and confinement, the sensuals walk the tightrope between spiritual purity and earthly desire. Undeniably conflicting, yet totally human forces of nature.

# Old Camden Cemetery – Chickens, Prostitutes, and Civil War Vets

Originally published Saturday, September 17, 2011
https://thecemeterytraveler.blogspot.com/2011/09/old–camden–cemetery–chickens.html

Just a short posting about an even shorter visit to the Old Camden Cemetery in Camden, New Jersey yesterday. I've driven past this small and forlorn weed–covered graveyard a number of times, usually as more of a landmark as I tried to find other, larger local cemeteries. But I was on my way home from work on a sunny September afternoon, and I thought I'd better check this place out before daylight savings ends.

So I cut off I–295 and descended into the depths of Camden. I drove under the PATCO High Speed Line railroad bridge near Mt. Ephraim Avenue and Mt. Vernon streets (a block from the cemetery), and slowed down to dodge potholes and hookers. I get the smile and wave from one of the latter. Ah, Camden. I pull up in front of the inner–city cemetery as ambulances rush by and a commuter train thunders overhead. Another woman is walking up the sidewalk toward me. I get my camera gear out of the trunk and head into the forlorn, dilapidated graveyard where she is sure not to follow. I think there must be an ordinance in Camden that prohibits a prostitute from propositioning you on consecrated ground. So she just leans on the fence and calls out to me. Responding politely in the negative, I went about photographing tombstones and she strolled away. This has happened to me before at other Camden cemeteries. Everyone needs a livelihood and I know this is an economically challenged area, but it's still a bit weird.

White marble headstones cocked at awkward angles litter the place. Large bags of trash had been unceremoniously tossed in the thigh–high weeds just inside the entrance (there is a fence, but no gate). Luckily I'm not in the habit of opening such trash bags; I was just reading up on the history of Old Camden Cemetery, and I came across this little gem posted by a visitor. Had I read this BEFORE walking the grounds, I may have … not!

"Adding a touch of the macabre are collections of plastic grocery bags filled with headless, mutilated chickens in full feather. At the center of one cluster of graves near a large tree was a two–foot–wide hole dug nearly three feet deep — for reasons one can only guess at."

It's no surprise that this city cemetery is in such deplorable condition. I mean, Camden can't even afford much of a police force – the Guardian Angels volunteered to supplement it last year (see "Guardian Angels take to NJ streets as cops dwindle" – https://www.reuters.com/article/us–camden–police/guardian–angels–take–to–nj–streets–as–cops–dwindle–idUSTRE7115GW20110202). So when you couple this with the fact that Camden has a 20% unemployment rate and is the "second most dangerous city in America," you begin to see why no discretionary funds are spent on the upkeep of its historic graveyards.

Old Camden Cemetery is, well, old. The burial ground was established in 1801, with burials ceasing in 1940. The place has become progressively more derelict over the past seventy years. It hasn't necessarily been abandoned, just uncared for. Though Camden's Department of Public Works is responsible for the cemetery, it's obvious that not much is done for its upkeep (I have seen the grass cut on occasion). In a city that cannot even afford to employ an adequate number of firefighters, teachers, or police, how could you expect money to be spent on an old cemetery?

As I walked the grounds, people would pass by outside the fence every few minutes and look curiously at me in the high weeds. Next time I'll carry a shovel over my shoulder – that'll REALLY give 'em something to ponder! The weeds were up to my elbows in many places, and I attempted to photograph a six–inch–long female praying mantis for a while (happy that I was not a male mantis – a female will usually eat the male's head while mating). A mantis will usually crawl up your arm if offered, but this one was a bit skittish (as was I, truthfully, but I was skittish about losing sight of my car). I followed the little critter around a tombstone, wondering if the ground below was piled with headless mantis bodies, when I realized that a big cemetery tree was now between me and my car. Stepping around it, I saw a couple of guys eying its open windows. At that point, my cell phone rang and they moved along.

I was shocked to later read that this (approximately) twenty acre cemetery has seen 11,000 burials! If you walk around the place, you'd guess there were only about 100 grave markers. Oddly, though, I stepped on many concealed (by weeds) headstone bases. What happened to the headstones? In the article, "Dead and Forgotten in Old Camden Cemetery" (http://historiccamdencounty.com/ccnews81.shtml), the authors state that in the past, when a headstone was knocked over, it was tossed into the back of a dump truck and dumped into the Delaware River off the Camden shoreline.

## United States Colored Troops

I guess I'm not surprised by this as Philadelphia did the same thing with an entire cemetery in 1958 (dumping 20,000 monuments from the condemned Monument Cemetery into the same river). I look out over this weed field, and see but a few tall monuments, some rusty cemetery fence, and one lonely granite memorial, the sad scene punctuated here and there by brightly–colored wildflowers. And speaking of colored, I came upon a marker for the grave of a Civil War veteran who was a member of the "U.S.C.T." — the 19th–century military acronym for "United States Colored Troops."

The existence of Private David Painter's grave is reason enough for the preservation of Old Camden Cemetery. The fact that he is buried here commemorates something of a culture change in America. The U.S.C.T. members were free African–Americans recruited by the Union Army to fight in the War Between the States. When they died, some communities rethought their racial segregation ideas, which had included burial prohibitions. In other words, blacks need to be buried separately from whites. Slowly, things began to change. Private Painter is buried in a cemetery that had previously barred the interment of blacks.

# SECTION 4:

# INTRODUCTION TO THE REST OF THE BOOK

This is an odd place for an introduction, I realize, but I felt I had to lay some groundwork first, and throw in some sex to go with the death. Now that you totally understand your motivation for reading about cemeteries and buying this book, you can vicariously enjoy them through my experiences (especially the ones about being in cemeteries at night!). Before we get to the rest of the book (which are edited blog postings from The Cemetery Traveler), allow me to tell you a bit about their genesis. It began with photography.

I began making photographs in cemeteries around 1997, when my (now ex-) wife began her affair with the neighbor. I needed something to do while my world collapsed. Perhaps it was subconsciously a form of meditation – a calming break from the outside world, a focus on my surroundings. As near as I can tell, my interest in cemetery photography (and later, writing about such dark tourism) was sparked by the angel statues I saw as I would drive by Holy Cross Cemetery in Yeadon, PA, on the outskirts of Philadelphia where I lived. When I first moved to this area from upstate New York, I lost four-years-worth of infrared landscape photography slides in a basement flood. I hadn't done much photography in the decade following that painful experience. All of a sudden, black and white angels seemed appealing. Not just because of the subject matter, but because of their total isolation from the natural environment. I never did resume doing landscape photography, because unlike upstate New York with its trees, hills, and waterfalls, Philadelphia has no nature (or so I felt at the time).

Since the late 1990s, I've visited hundreds of cemeteries and graveyards (the latter, technically, are those burial grounds in churchyards). I photographed angel statues, predominantly, for about ten years before I began photographing other dead things and documenting my experiences by writing the Cemetery Traveler blog. To paraphrase Henry David Thoreau, I've traveled widely in Philadelphia, since this happens to be where I live. But I've been all across America, even spent a bit of time in Italy. I've learned a lot about the dead, as well as the living. The greater Philadelphia area has literally hundreds of cemeteries, both large and small. The more I hung around in them, the more interested I became in what was written on the headstones, the people who work there, the history, architecture, and burial practices. My interests evolved from the macabre to the more intellectual. Mainly, I learned a lot about myself. I've also learned about what drives people toward volunteerism, I've learned about the Civil War, I've even gotten laid – all because of cemeteries. Through my blog, I allow you to join me as I explore life through death.

For years, people kept asking me, "Why do you take pictures in cemeteries?" For years, I honestly had no answer. Since they kept asking me, I thought I should come up with some cogent and succinct, yet plausible answers to the question. These people were buying my work at art shows and wanted the story. I would like to think that my photographs stand alone on their artistic merit, but as my daughter (who attended art school) tells me, "People are more interested in the artist's *story*, than the work itself."

I've exhibited in galleries and sold many fine art prints of images I've captured in cemeteries. I've been doing this since the late 1990s. I enjoy my own work, and to have someone actually want to purchase a print is very humbling. Early on, I was not prepared for the fact that buyers often felt inclined to tell me why they bought a certain piece. I never asked. Sometimes the stories were funny, e.g., "My girlfriend needs this over the head of her bed," other times more sobering, e.g., "This angel reminds me of the one standing over my two-year-old child's grave." I wished that I could say something that profound. It is difficult for me to describe why I see beauty in cemeteries, as I'm not a very introspective person. To give an example: a woman once asked me what I liked most about John Donne's poetry. I said, "Mainly, the words."

I think my work is an attempt to come to terms with mortality, but honestly, there are times when I exude a profound inner shallowness - perhaps, like the photographer Gary Winogrand, I simply want to see what a particular scene looks like as a photograph.

Why photograph cemeteries and not dogs, people, or sailboats? Well, as the artist Georgia O'Keefe said, "I paint flowers because they're cheaper than models and they don't move." Cemeteries are usually free to get in, the owners allow photography, and headstones are inanimate objects. When you talk about shooting a "still life," they don't get any stiller than a graveyard. I actually like the ordered geometry of cemeteries, the rectangular headstones, the house-like mausoleums, the statuary. I also have an appreciation for the fencing, the borders, walls, and gates. Fences are easily scaled, and from time to time I am reminded that these barriers are not so much for security as they are to keep the living from having to think about dying.

This is my first collection of Cemetery Traveler essays, from blogs I've been writing since 2010. At this point I have about 250 from which to choose. You'll get about twenty-five hand-chosen essays in this book. The postings are only categorized by date on the blog, so the book gives me a chance to organize them in a more meaningful fashion. So for instance, if you're more interested in abandoned cemeteries than the supernatural, you can just go to that section.

And speaking of the supernatural, Stephen King, in his book, "On Writing," says that for the most part, he lets a story tell itself, i.e., he creates it as he writes it. He rarely develops the story from an outline, and rarely knows how it will end before he writes the ending, when he solves the problem, as it were. He simply begins with a situation, and that develops into a story. That's how I write my blogs, very "stream of consciousness." I write from memory – sometimes the same day as my adventure, sometimes ten years later. I try to be as factual as possible, given the circumstances. That said, I've had some "otherworldly" experiences in graveyards, which you'll read about in the following section. I've never captured "orbs" on film or seen ghosts, but I figure I owe that to my basic tenet, "The more you believe in them the more they'll try to get you." However – I have had a few inexplicable experiences that have no earthly explanation that I can discern.

If you are reading this book, you get two extra essays that were not published on the blog – the introductory piece, "*Poisoning the Well*" (the working title of which was "Scarred for Life") and this *Introduction*, all of which explain how and why I became interested in cemeteries. If you're wondering, the essays in this book won't be taken exactly from my blog – I need to remove some of the references to the many photographs in the blog. The blog is based on photographic journeys through cemeteries. In this book, I can only use one lead monochrome image for each essay. If you want to see the many photos in color, please go to the blog (https://thecemeterytraveler.blogspot.com/) and type a keyword (e.g. "zombies," for instance) from the essay of interest into the "Search" box in the upper left portion of the page, and that will take you right to the original.

The essays in this book allow me to say want I want about death. In a nutshell, the book is about my awkward search for my own place in the larger human family. Mortality has a lot to do with this. After I crossed over to the wrong side of fifty, I suppose mortality began to bear down on me. I also began thinking of the imminent death of my loved ones, including you, dear reader, and writing it all down while a portion of my life is still in front of me. I'm writing two hours before going under the knife for cancer surgery.

# SECTION 5:

# THE UNEXPLAINED

Okay, you bought a book about graveyards, you expect scary stories. Well, here they are. Just remember: the more you believe in them, the more they'll try to get you.

*"I can remember always being afraid of cemeteries as a young girl. I don't know why, but I would hold my breath whenever we drove past a grave yard."*
– Susan S.

# The Voices Within

Originally published Sunday, April 3, 2011
https://thecemeterytraveler.blogspot.com/2011/04/locked-in-and-climbing-out.html

When it comes to blood–chilling fear, being locked in a cemetery isn't quite on par with public speaking, but it is close. Still, I'd guess most people would opt not to be locked in a cemetery, given the choice. In my cemetery roamings, I've been locked in a few times. And believe me, it's not something you get used to.

The main reason I now pay close attention to closing times is because of an adventure my brother and I had at Woodlawn Cemetery in the north Bronx, NYC. This was maybe in the summer of 2002, as far as I can recall, and my first time being locked in. I had convinced him to take the train with me from Philadelphia to the Bronx to go shooting in this grand old Victorian cemetery. It's all the way at the north end of a subway/elevated line at the Woodlawn stop, a pretty rough neighborhood. Worth the effort, though, as it is certainly one of the most elaborate and picturesque cemeteries in the country. Back then, it was my own precious discovery.

This being my first time at Woodlawn, I mistook the cemetery's rear gate on Jerome Avenue for the main gate, (which is actually on Webster Avenue and East 233rd Street, clear on the opposite side of this huge 400–acre cemetery). The Jerome Avenue gate and wrought iron fencing were about 10 feet high. My brother made special note of that, and commented on the 4:30 closing time (he's such a worrywart).

We spent hours being awestruck by the amazing statues and mausoleums, especially the angels. One of the most fabulous memorials I have ever seen is the defeated Woodlawn angel shown in the image above. Years later a woman saw it in one of my shows and said, "It's so sad even the angels are crying." I shot most of a roll of film of this singular statue, from various angles, bracketing exposures, and having my brother hold tree branches out of my way. I needed to get this down; the north Bronx is too far from home for a return trip.

As it turns out, the image you see above was actually taken on a second trip some months later, as my developer messed up that entire roll of film–it came out severely overexposed (couldn't have been my fault, right?). All the other film I shot that day was fine, it was just this one roll, for some reason!

So my brother and I spent about four hours at Woodlawn photographing the magnificent statuary and toward the end of the day, we began to make our way back toward the gate. Not far from the exit, I had my head turned by the magnificent Belmont mausoleum. This architectural wonder is a full–scale replica of the Chapel of St. Hubert in France's famed Loire valley (where the best wine comes from, I might add). It was designed by Leonardo Da Vinci in the "Gothic Flamboyant" style in the early 1500s. Da Vinci's remains were placed in a sarcophagus in this original chapel. So this ain't no ordinary mausoleum. Who could afford something like this? Or go to such a design extreme? Its residents, Oliver and Alva Belmont, certainly had the money. Oliver Belmont was a millionaire (the oldest horse race in the Triple Crown, the Belmont Stakes, is named for August Belmont, his father), and his wife Alva had enormous personal wealth as well, having previously married into the Vanderbilt family.

After we exhausted our film on the gargoyles and flying buttresses (I don't really know what those are but I always wanted to say "flying buttresses"), we realized it was 4:45! Aahhhh! To the gate!...... What?! CLOSED!!! Ahhh!!!

After some howls and imprecations on my brother's part (directed mainly toward me), I took the predicament into consideration and figured it was possible to climb up the inside of the gate and down the other side. With my camera bag on my shoulder, I scaled up the inside of the gate, thankful for the built–in footholds of ornamental wrought iron, over the top and down the front. Getting Tim over the gate was quite another story – my poor brother had a horrendous time! He cursed me coast to coast during both his ascent and descent. At one point, he was sitting on top of the closed gate with me outside trying to convince him that a safe dismount was indeed possible. I was conscious of cars on the highway slowing down to look at us, with the drivers probably thinking, "Why are they trying to get out? In this neighborhood, it's certainly safer inside that cemetery!" But he got out, with me jamming his feet into footholds he couldn't see. Took about a half hour in the hot setting summer sun. To cool him down (in more ways than one) I bought him a few beers at the biker bar under the el stop across the street. Then we took the long series of train rides home.

Had we known there was a front entrance, we certainly would have tried to get to it to see if there were any people about (I found out later that the main entrance was literally one mile away through the center of the cemetery – the place is that big!). As an aside, I came to find out even later that the gate we climbed over used to be quite famous. The Jerome Avenue gate of Woodlawn Cemetery was the site of a clandestine meeting related to the "Crime of the Century," the supposed kidnapping of the Lindbergh baby in 1932. One evening, a police officer reported seeing a man sitting on top of the closed gate talking with someone on the sidewalk outside the gate. These men were believed to be Charles Lindbergh's agent (Dr. John Condon) and the kidnapper/extortionist. It is believed that the ransom money dropoff related to the Lindbergh baby kidnapping occurred at this very gate!

## The Return Trip

Since none of my images of the Weeping Angel came out, I was determined to have another go at it. The statue is just so powerful, I had to realize my own vision of it. I was on a mission – as the banner over Alva Belmont's crypt says, 'Failure is Impossible'. So I planned a solo trip a few months later. I knew when the sun would be illuminating that particular part of the cemetery and figured I needed to be in there after 4:30 pm (obviously after the gates were closed). I would wander around Woodlawn for a couple hours, allow myself to be locked in, spend as much time as I needed to make the photographs, then climb out. So my second experience being locked in a cemetery was elective. During the planning stage, a woman I knew suggested we go together, take mushrooms, and spend the night in the cemetery. Can you imagine having a bad trip in a cemetery?! Crawling around licking tombstones (or worse)? I think I'd rather eat bees. So I went solo.

**Voices in the Cemetery**

I like to think that I'm not superstitious. However, I am susceptible to suggestion. I returned to Woodlawn by myself to photograph the amazing life–sized statue (angels are the same size as us, right?) you see in the image above. I scheduled my trip with the intent of being locked in the cemetery. The reason? The lighting is better at dusk. Photographers typically shoot at the edges of the day, in order for the sun to produce as much shadow as possible. Helps to create the illusion of a 3D image.

So I go to Woodlawn on the appointed day, spend a couple hours shooting around the cemetery, find the statue (which I've since titled, "End of Miles"), then hide and wait until the gates are closed (and locked). Having done this before, I didn't see a problem with scaling the 10–foot wrought iron gate to get out.

When the setting sun was in the correct position, I made the photographs of the statue, one of which you see here. All that remained was to make my way through the cemetery to the rear gate, scale it, then have a nice cold one at the bar under the Woodlawn el stop across the street.

On my way I stopped to photograph a statue. As I was looking through the viewfinder of my camera to line up the shot, I distinctly saw a long furry ringed tail disappear behind a bush! I left my camera on the tripod and walked over to, and around, the bush. Nothing! No hole, no animal. I could think of only one thing – The Bronx Zoo! What made this even more disturbing, was the deafening quiet of the cemetery.

Victorian Garden Cemeteries like Woodlawn were landscaped by architects in the 1800s with the purpose of maintaining contemplative serenity through floral beauty and silence. While in such an idyllic paradise, you simply cannot see or hear anything – not trains, planes, or automobiles! The silence is very much with you when you know you're the only person locked in the cemetery...

Already rattled from the tail sighting, I packed up my gear and continued (but this time briskly) walking toward the locked entrance gate. As I walked along, I passed a monument adorned with a life–sized statue of a seated woman with two children at her knee. I read the inscription as I passed – it was something like, "Dedicated to a mother who loved her children." As I said the word 'children' in my mind, there was a loud audible baby's cry! My blood froze as I ran for the gate! I never photographed that particular statue – I was 2-S (too scared).

## Locked in the Cemetery!

Originally published Saturday, September 4, 2010
https://thecemeterytraveler.blogspot.com/2013/04/ghosts-in-receiving-vault.html

Whenever I photograph in a cemetery, I pay attention to an important sign at the entrance—the one that tells me when "Closing Time" is. Minor detail, but neglecting this has gotten me into some tough scrapes. Not that I'm scared of being locked in a cemetery—walking by a dialysis clinic should be more frightening, you know? All those people on the other side of that wall will probably be dead in a month.

Ignoring the possibility of being attacked by the living dead, getting yourself locked in a cemetery poses a certain inconvenience—especially if you're locked in with your car. At least as a pedestrian, you can climb over the wall...before they release the dogs, that is. Who am I kidding? I don't want to be locked in a cemetery under any circumstances!

Back around 2005, I was photographing in the Woodlands Cemetery in West Philadelphia. This is an oasis of fifty-three partially wooded acres surrounded by city — The University of Pennsylvania and The University of the Sciences, mostly. Its a quietly creepy kind of place, with the sculpted hills blocking out most of the city noise. The 1853 Charter of Woodlands Cemetery boasts:

*"... Here amid nature's beautiful works, embellished by taste, is offered the right of sepulture in perpetuity. Here in a dry and gravelly soil the decaying bodies of the dead may securely moulder into kindred dust, with an abundant vegetation and free winds to absorb and dissipate all noxious effluvia."*

Poetic, don't you think? Certainly not a place you want to get locked up in. Anyway, I vaguely glanced at the closing time sign on the entrance gate when I drove in — 4:30 p.m. I spent a few hours shooting, when I noticed an old pickup truck drive by, heading toward the maintenance garage. I glanced at my watch. Hmmm. 4:20 p.m. Best pack up my gear. I drove to the entrance and, to my horror, the gate was chained shut! My first inclination was to panic. Which I did, quite effortlessly, as I recall, but then remembered the pickup truck. I drove at amazing speed toward the maintenance garage and found a man sitting in the driver's seat of the idling truck. I drove up alongside him and asked as casually as I could if he could let me out. He looked at me and with the few teeth he had, laughed and said, "That's the only way to get you people out of here!" He did let me out. As I quickly exited the cemetery, I noticed this decoration on the main gate—an hourglass with wings! Time flies, get it? What better symbol to remind one of closing time! Needless to say, I now pay closer attention to closing times.

Obviously its more than inconvenience that makes us prefer to not be locked in a cemetery. We're taught at a young age that there are no such thing as monsters. It can't simply be fear of mortality. What then strikes fear in our hearts? The possibilities are only limited by our imagination....
A friend of mine once worked in a cemetery and told me that she didn't believe there were any 'bad' spirits haunting cemeteries. If a person happened to die a horrible death, the person's ghost would hang around the place where the death occurred, not the body's final resting place. We laugh at comments like this with much bravado sometimes, either due to ignorance or because we're secretly afraid. Sometimes we think we're above all that "superstitious nonsense." I often recall something I heard a mother tell her three–year–old daughter at a gallery opening in Manhattan for an exhibit of nineteenth century "spiritualist" photography. It was a telling comment on how our views and beliefs change over time. She gestured around the room at all the hanging photographs and said, "This was all before people knew any better."

I am happy to report that cemeteries are becoming more in tune with people's visitation habits. It seem to me that in the span of time from 1998 to about 2010, many more people are visiting cemeteries for reasons other than to mourn a lost soul. They are, in fact, becoming popular tourist destinations, at least the old Victorian ones are. One consequence of this, I'm sure, is the easing of the "locked gate" situation.

I was amazed to note around 2015 that West Laurel Cemetery in Bala Cynwyd, Pennsylvania, has a sign at the exit which says something like, "If gate is closed, blow horn." The sound triggers the gate opening mechanism so you can get out! Ah, technology! I visited another cemetery, Holy Cross, in Yeadon, Pennsylvania, during a snowstorm in the winter of 2017 (Hey, if you haven't photographed a cemetery in a snowstorm, you don't know what you're missing!). The sign said closing time was 4:30. It was 4 pm when I pulled in through the gates driving my wife's Toyota RAV4 (my Saab convertible is terrible in snow, so I was prepared). One of the office workers was shoveling snow off his car when I pulled up beside him, hoping the place was not closing early. I asked him, and he said, "We're open 'til 4:30. But if you do get locked in, just call 911. The Yeadon Police have a key to the gate." Now that, my friends, is progress!

## Zombie Chill

Originally published Thursday, July 19, 2012
https://thecemeterytraveler.blogspot.com/2012/07/zombie-chill.html

I finally made my way onto the set of a zombie movie. I've had several opportunities over the years, but last weekend the planets were finally in alignment. My friend, who works at Laurel Hill Cemetery in Philadelphia, rung me up to tell me that a movie company was filming zombie scenes that night in the graveyard. Would I want to come by? Ha! Does a zombie eat folks in the woods?!

When I arrived, the actors were getting their makeup applied – fake brains oozing out of the top of baseball caps, torn clothes, fake blood spattered over flesh. After a bit of this fascinating scene, we walked through the cemetery to the place where the scenes would be shot. A generator was running, power cables lay in the grass and a few giant "barn door" style movie lights were on. This part of the cemetery looked quite eerie with the tombstones lit up white and the background pitch black.

We chatted a bit about his previous night's work (which happened to be on Friday the thirteenth!) helping to set up for an outdoor screening of Ed Wood's Plan 9 From Outer Space and a 1937 court-ordered exhumation film made at Laurel Hill Cemetery. The latter a fascinating story involving a will valued at twenty million dollars that was thought to be buried inside a woman's coffin (someone had actually found the film at a local flea market!). Believe it or not, nearly a thousand people showed up for movie night at the cemetery!

In comparison, this mid-July zombie evening was very quiet. It was also quite warm, about eighty degrees. The sky was cloudy, and their reflection of the distant city lights gave a luster of midday to objects below … well, maybe not quite that bright. It was light enough at 10 p.m., however, that you didn't need a flashlight to navigate your way around the cemetery.

My friend is Laurel Hill's night man – he's the guy called upon to do all the night work at the cemetery. Night work? There are many people who request night access (when the gates are locked) to do model shoots, music videos, movies, and paranormal investigations. Frank lets them in, shows them around, helps get them set up, and is available for any issues that might come up. He also lives on the grounds (well, in a house on the grounds) and serves as night watchman for the cemetery. So he's seen a lot. As we chatted, waiting for the film crew and actors to arrive, I was thinking I should've brought of few beers, it was so hot. About that moment, I felt an unmistakable coldness on my left elbow. It was brief, about two seconds, but I felt it. There were no breezes that night. I stopped Frank in mid-sentence and told him, after which he replied, "The paranormal investigators always say this is the most active part of the cemetery." Out of seventy-eight acres, odd that the zombie folk chose this spot. In all my cemetery travels, this is the first time I ever experienced the "ghostly chill," which I did not feel again that evening. I've looked up the "rational" explanations for the cold sensation, and none of them wholly explains what I felt. I had no goosebumps, and I wasn't scared (consciously or subconsciously). It was not a cold breeze, as I felt nothing on my legs (I was wearing shorts and a T-shirt).

The rest of the evening was uneventful, as far as ghosts were concerned. I was intrigued by the fact that the cinematographer (videographer?) was using a professional-grade DSLR with video capability, which seems to be the equipment of choice even for some high-budget motion picture projects. After my initial fascination with being on a movie set and seeing zombies wore off, it was all rather tedious. Multiple takes of every scene kind of wears on you, as an observer, anyway. Still, it was a bit weird having zombies come up to me in a graveyard asking if I was afraid …. I was actually afraid they would continue telling me bad zombie jokes.

The more interesting part of the experience was seeing parts of the cemetery artificially lit with movie lights (of a temperature balanced for daylight), which made it apparent to a photographer (me) how cinematographers use light to create mood. The kind of creepy thing was seeing all the night beetles crawling up the marble obelisks all around us. Every once in a while, one would land on a hot light and be slowly incinerated – Bzzzzzttt!! The first time I saw and heard this, I thought the light was burning up, there was that much smoke! I alerted a member of the crew, who went over to examine the burning hot surface of the light. He picked it up by its stand, shook out the beetle parts, and the show went on.

I shot a few of the scenes that were being filmed, being careful not to click my shutter after the "Quiet on the set!" proclamation was made. Having my camera with me made me feel somewhat official, like it was a press pass or something. It's interesting how the camera, as writer Susan Sontag puts it, can make everyone a tourist in other people's reality – and eventually in one's own.

# Ghosts in the Receiving Vault?

Originally published Thursday, April 25, 2013
https://thecemeterytraveler.blogspot.com/2013/04/ghosts-in-receiving-vault.html

You know how ghost hunters always say their cameras stopped working when they were trying to take a photograph in some spirit-active location? Well, it finally happened to me. You would think that after fifteen years of photographing in cemeteries, I would have experienced this more often.

Last weekend I was out at Mount Moriah Cemetery in West Philly for a cleanup day. About twenty people were working in Section 21. Bright sunny cool spring day, not the kind of ambiance you would think would attract ghosts, but I suppose my guard was down. The old receiving vault is in this section next to a crumbling mausoleum, unmarked and unassuming. Big pile of dirt in front of the doorless entrance, with about a one-foot high opening at the top (seen in photo above). Someone at some point bulldozed the entrance closed. I was told the vault is just filled with plastic flowers taken from graves over the years – graveyard trash. I figured, hey, it may still make an interesting photograph.

So I climbed up the bank of dirt and rocks and peered in. Piles of old plastic flowers alright, of the funeral arrangement type – grave blankets, as they say. Set my DSLR to forced flash and pointed it inside. Hit the shutter release and ... nothing. Pulled the camera back out into the light, checked all the settings. The focus-setting strobe wasn't strobing to set the focus, for some reason. So I set the focus and locked it (an auto focus camera will hunt for something on which to focus, and if it doesn't find something, it won't let you click the shutter). Still wouldn't work. Huh.

Pulled the camera out of the receiving vault and tried it in the daylight. Worked fine. Buggerall. I know this camera (Canon Rebel XTi) like the back of my hand. Why wouldn't it work? As I climbed down the embankment, I realized a woman had been watching me from down on the road. As I approached, she said, "Flash wouldn't work, would it?" I was stunned. "What…?," I said. To which she replied, "Happened to me too. It's because of the serial killer that was in there." She proceeded to enlighten me about H.H. Holmes, America's first known serial killer. After he was hung for murder in Philadelphia in 1896, his body – with the noose still around its neck – was supposedly temporarily held in the Mount Moriah receiving vault.

From what I've heard, Holmes, whose real name was Herman Webster Mudgett, was set to be buried in Holy Cross Cemetery, Yeadon, PA, a mile or so away from Mount Moriah. After he was executed (at Moyamensing Prison, which is now an ACME in South Philly where I live), Holy Cross had second thoughts about the burial on its property. Perhaps because of the unusual requirements that Mudgett be buried in an unusually deep grave with his body encased in cement inside his coffin, it took a bit of time for Holy Cross to finally accept the burial. I assume Mudgett paid ahead of time for this elaborate interment, and maybe went to this trouble because he was afraid that others would do the same to his body as he had done to so many others. He reputedly killed 200 people (he was convicted of four murders), many in his custom-designed "murder castle" in Chicago during the 1893 Columbian Exposition. At least some of his victims had their flesh boiled off their bones so that he could sell their fully articulated (rebuilt) skeletons to medical schools.

But back to that day at Mount Moriah. As I was leaving Section 21, I drove my car a short distance, stopped and got out. Wanted to get a long view of the receiving vault. That's when, unbeknownst to me, my flip phone found its way out of my belt holster and became intimate with the ground.

I got back into my car and drove around to the 1855 brownstone gatehouse, where I stopped to get out and take a few more photos. A car passed mine going in the opposite direction, driven by no one I recognized. As I came back to my car, I realized my cell phone was gone. Damn. High speed thinking, swearing, then praying – you know how that goes. Ran back to the weeds where I had crouched around the crumbling gatehouse -

nothing. Nothing but a deer tick on my pant leg, that is, which I flicked away. Funny, first time I'd ever seen one. Maybe my luck is changing for the worse. Man, if I had dropped my phone somewhere back in the woods - well, it could be anywhere. That's when it hit me - I just used it to check the time after I shot the road-level view of the receiving vault. Maybe it fell out when I got back into my car?

I turned my car around, drove back down the dirt road to Section 21 and saw my phone lying in two pieces in the road. Either I drove over it or that other car did. I put the phone back together and miraculously, it worked! Got in my car to head home, thanking my lucky stars, when the brake failure warning light illuminated on my dashboard. Coincidences or Holmes' influence?

The next day, Sunday, was a nice day as well. I decided to make a solo trip back to Mount Moriah. However, the main reason I wanted to go back was because the light was about the same as the previous day and I wanted to get a few wide angle views of the section of the cemetery up behind the receiving vault. There were some large monuments in the woods there which had been knocked off their foundations by huge fallen trees. This was, for me, a previously unexplored portion of this massively overgrown cemetery and I wanted to get back there with my trusty camera. In the back of my mind, I was curious about whether or not I could get those shots inside the receiving vault.

After climbing through the tangle of trees, brush, and sharply-thorned rose bushes, I got the photographs I was after. I emerged from the woods to the sound of a chainsaw. I joke with people that Mount Moriah is the only cemetery where you don't have to be frightened when you hear a chainsaw. Its just volunteers working in conjunction with the Friends of Mount Moriah Cemetery, Inc., felling invasive trees on this spectacularly overgrown property. In this case it was just my friend Ken ripping through some small trees down the hill, giving yet another monument its freedom. So I climbed down the hill toward Ken and the receiving vault to give the inside photo another go. When I got to the small hole at the top of the blocked doorway, I pointed my camera inside and the flash worked every time. Any mode I dialed in, camera worked just fine. Plastic flowers on a hard dirt floor, nothing more. Or maybe what was there yesterday, decided to be at Holy Cross today.

## Epilogue

Years after I wrote this blog, fast-forward to 2017 – H.H. Holmes has become almost a household name (well, at least among those true crime enthusiasts who are into serial killers). Holmes' body was disinterred from its unmarked grave in Holy Cross Cemetery. There was a History Channel series called "American Ripper," based on Holmes' great-great-grandchildren's feelings that perhaps Holmes had cheated the gallows and paid to have another body buried in his place. Another theory was that Holmes was actually Jack the Ripper! The grave was excavated, the remains retrieved, DNA and dental analysis done. Turned out that Mudgett was just another serial killer, not the infamous Ripper. It was verified via dental records that the body, which was later re-buried at Holy Cross, was indeed that of Mudgett. Based on video footage from the news and the documentary, a friend of mine and I found the excavated site where Mudgett is buried. Knowing the horrors that he, the "*Devil in the White City,*" inflicted on unsuspecting victims, I was conflicted in my emotions looking down on that grave. That guy was pure evil.

Note: "*Devil in the White City,*" (2004, Vintage) is an historical novel by Erik Larson, which chronicles H. H. Holmes' killing escapades in Chicago during the 1893 World's Fair.

# Haunted Texas Graveyard

Originally published Friday, July 1, 2011
http://thecemeterytraveler.blogspot.com/2011/07/many-apologies-to-my-readers-for-being.html

Many apologies to my readers for being tardy with my weekly blog. I just flew in from Texas, and my arms are really tired. Sorry, old joke. So, the question is, are there cemeteries in Texas? You bet. No one ever talks about them, those graveyards of the old west, except for maybe Boot Hill (and that's in Tombstone, Arizona, anyway). I can unequivocally say that there are cemeteries in Texas – simple ones, abandoned ones, even opulent Victorian ones, family cemeteries, and haunted graveyards. I found some of each right around San Antonio, where I was teaching for a few days this past weekend. What I want to write about here is one in particular, a haunted one – the Loma China Cemetery south of San Antonio, in Bexar County.

In preparation for my trip, I surfed the Web for interesting local cemeteries. Through a Facebook Friend, I found a gem of an entry from lostdestinations.com that refers to a Chinese graveyard. It instructed one to go down Zarzamora and after you pass the Route 410 loop, the road makes a slight turn to the right and on the right is a big white cross. Quickly flash your headlights five times and listen for people talking and look for white apparitions moving around the small graveyard. The site showed a handmade sign from the graveyard that reads "No Witchcraft".

Your favorite Cemetery Traveler could not resist a temptation like that! In fact the "Chinese Graveyard" (also known as Loma China Cemetery) was my first stop after deplaning, as they say. Well, actually, my first stop was to check out the local cuisine. Munching on alligator nuggets and frogs legs, rockin' to Mexican radio, I headed south through San Antonio last Friday afternoon.

About the weather: I wrote in my last blog that the coldest weather I've ever experienced was on Sodus Bay, New York, on Lake Ontario. Well, I just experienced the torrential Texan sun and I have never been so hot in my life! Jesus H. Chrissmus, how do you people TOLERATE that? A hundred and seventeen degrees in Lubbock this weekend?! San Antone was so hot that birds were bursting into flame as they flew through the sun beams reflected off the tall, glass-windowed office buildings.* The digital temp readout on my rental car's dashboard blanked out after it hit a hundred, it just started flashing out of range. Thank the gods for air conditioning!

Anyway, Zarzamora street runs north-south through San Antonio. After crossing 410 south of the city, it heads off into rural Texas as a sparsely traveled four-lane lost highway. About a quarter mile from that intersection, I came upon the small graveyard on the right side of the road. I pulled into the space in front of the gate (oddly, there was only room for one car to park) and got out to survey the opportunity. It looked like new cyclone fence had been erected around the old entrance gate since the lostdestinations photos were taken (the author's account was published in the book, Weird Texas).

At the top of the gate in faded paint you could read something like "Guzman Burial Ground." Given the fact that I didn't see a "big white cross," I began to wonder if I was in the right place. The gate was locked but not insurmountable. Still, if I don't have to scale a fence, I won't, so I checked for an opening. The left side of the cemetery was fenced off to an industrial equipment site and the right side was open to woods. The front fence on the right actually ended at the woods, so all I had to do was go around the fence, climb over a pile of old cemetery decorations, and enter the grounds (I once met a sculptor who creates new works of art from discarded grave decorations – just thought you should know that!) . I didn't see any "No Trespassing" signs, so I didn't feel like I was. I grabbed my DSLR and a couple Holgas and went inside.

It was a cemetery alright, but a very meager and informal one. The grounds themselves were only about sixty feet wide, maybe two city blocks deep. Certainly not the type of affluent cemetery that would invite grave robbers, though such an atrocity did happen here in 2009 (http://strangesanantonio.blogspot.com/2009/02/digging-up-dead.html).

There were tombstones, but not very elaborate ones, wooden crosses with names carved into them, cement grave borders mixed with sea shells (a la New Orleans). Many of the graves on the left were members of the Guzman family, which made me think the place was a private family burial ground. There are some Chinese graves on the right, but not really that many. Those had mementos and ornaments around the stones, along with brightly colored plastic flowers, which could have been new, could have been twenty years old, hard to say. There were headstones as recent as 1996, some so old you couldn't read the dates.

I really was thinking I was in the wrong place until I came upon this sign in the weeds, amidst old beer bottles and other trash. It's the same sign you see on the lostdestinations site. Toward the back of the cemetery I found a concrete bench on which was painted "Loma China Cemetary" [sic], which confirmed that I had found the right place. To my utter disappointment, the "No Witchcraft" sign was nowhere to be seen.

When I eventually made it to the back of the graveyard where the bench is, I found some old headstones covered in cacti, all shaded by a couple great old cemetery trees – you know, the kind of gnarly old things that seem to only grow in cemeteries. Across from them was a grave with a rectangular wooden headstone with a painted plaster angel on it. The angel's face was so startlingly lifelike that as I was photographing it, I half expected it to open its eyes. Creepy.

The absence of traffic on four-lane Zanzamora street was weird. Even though the Chinese Cemetery bordered some sort of construction equipment supply place on one side, all was quiet there on Friday afternoon. I comforted my uneasiness with the fact that other than the tourists, the locals must be too smart to go out in this weather. At a 114 degree 'real feel' temperature, I was sweating like crazy. It dripped off my sunburned face as I lay on my back in the sand, photographing the cacti-covered headstones. Red ants were everywhere – I shook them off my Holgas. I felt that if the cemetery were really haunted, this is exactly where you would experience the weirdness. But I thought the ghosties wouldn't be around in broad daylight in this heat. Like, even if you were to see one, it would be lying in the shade, weakly holding up a small sign that said "Boo." With the creepy angel face and the painted bench behind me, I thought I felt something inside the leg of my shorts.

Now, in all candor, I must say I had forgotten all about rattlesnakes. It wasn't until days later as I'm writing this blog that it even occurs to me to look that up! Who knew Texas has TEN varieties of rattlesnake? More than any other state besides Arizona? Had I known this, I would've exercised a bit more caution.

But no serpents, thank you very much. However, as I looked down, I saw six-inch lizards scurrying everywhere! Yaahhhh !!!! Jump up, shake pant leg. Nothing. Wait – the lizards were actually all … heading for the angel head. This is too weird. Maybe time to go. I gathered up all my camera gear and was ready to head out of there when I realized the lens cap was missing from my DSLR. I had been snapping it on between shots to keep the sweat from dripping onto the lens. Now, years ago I used to lose these things left and right, until I started buying those elastic bands that stretch around the lens base with the button at the end of a tether that sticks to the lens cap. You pop the cap off and drop it – the tether lets it dangle until you're ready to put it back on the lens. Haven't lost a cap in ten years. Until now, that is. In fact, the elastic band was gone too!

With some reluctance, I retraced my steps and searched for about twenty minutes, to no avail. It wasn't like it fell into bushes or tall grass, its just basically sand there. A four-inch black lens cap should be easy to locate, but the sweat was pouring off me and my glasses were a mess. Under the unrelenting Texas sun, I felt like that line from the Fountains of Wayne song, "And the sun is beating me senseless, I feel defenseless like a dying lamb…." I gave up and headed back to the car. Threw my gear in the trunk with the suitcases and pulled away from Loma China Cemetery.

A mere twenty feet down Zarzamora I see one of those roadside memorials, you know, plastic flowers and stuffed animals in remembrance of someone who died in a car wreck. At some point I intend to blog about them, so I pulled off the road into the drainage ditch to grab a few photos. As the memory card in my DLSR was almost full I decided to change it. I popped the full one out, and it fell between the seat and shifting console! After spewing some imprecations, I moved the electric seat forward, got out and crawled into the back and fished around for it. Finally got it. Jeez Louise.

I went down to shoot the memorial, and the sign spelling "Brother" was facing the wrong direction, so I clambered around to the other side. I grabbed a handful of what I thought was just bracken, to pull it out of the way so I could photograph the front of the memorial, and my left hand was bloodied by dozens of invisible thorns! Holy shit, did that hurt!

I began to seriously think the spirits of Loma China Cemetery were messing with me. Bugger all, man, it was worth it! Bad luck notwithstanding, I saw a cool graveyard and maybe got some decent photographs. So off I went to check into my hotel.

After a shower a few hours later, I began unpacking my bags. When I got to the bottom of one of my locked suitcases, guess what was in there? My lens cap with the tether! WTF!? – ghosts that like to play parlor tricks? I guess it was a sign that they really could harm me if they wanted to! But that wasn't the end of the weirdness. My bad luck streak continued for six days.

One of the reasons I'm late posting this blog is because after writing it the first time, my laptop decided to "Restart," and I apparently did not save my document. So what you're reading is Version 2.0 (which reminds me to hit "Save" at this point…). As I left San Antonio, my plane was delayed so I nearly missed my connecting flight in Houston (remember those TV commercials with O.J. Simpson running through the airport?). Upon my arrival in Philadelphia, the announcement that it was 79 degrees and cloudy made it seem like paradise compared to what I had endured over the past four days! Texans must be a hardy people. So around midnight, in relatively high spirits, the airport shuttle dropped me off in front of my car – which had a flat tire.

When I got into work the next day, I noticed that the hard drive with all my blogs and years of photographs was missing. No big deal – I had disconnected it, put it in my bag and took it home with me last week. I spent the last several days looking for that damned thing, everywhere! I had given it up for lost. My bad luck ended (I hope) yesterday when I walked into my office and found the drive under a sheet of paper. Now, this is one of those instances where it wasn't there the LAST four times you looked there, but now it IS there. Plausible explanation? My wife thinks it must have decided that I had worked hard enough to find it, so it decided to reappear. The quantum physicists might say that it's waveform had just temporarily collapsed. My advice? If you decide to visit Loma China Cemetery, be sure to take your lucky amulet or anti-witchcraft talisman with you.

* Just kidding about the birds bursting into flame.

**Epilogue**

It was really difficult finding information on this cemetery on the internet before I visited, but when I returned home and searched for "Guzman Burial Ground" (the words painted on the entrance sign), I found something that explained a bit of the place's history.

In a 2009 interview, local citizen Joey Guzman says that the Chinese Cemetery is in fact his family's private burial ground, which had originated over a hundred years ago. And the Chinese connection? The ghostly apparition you supposedly see when you flash your headlights? Well, supposedly a great uncle of his was in love with a Chinese woman. Guzman, who maintains the cemetery, says his great-grandfather forbade the great uncle from seeing his true love. Guzman believes that what is now a graveyard was a rendezvous spot for his ancestor and his Asian lover. (https://ghostcitytours.com/san-antonio/haunted-places/chinese-graveyard/)

This was the Romeo and Juliet story of Bexar County at the time. The woman, whose name has not been passed down to us, was reportedly a Chinese immigrant. The great uncle was killed while on his horse, as they were both struck by lightning. Folklore says his Asian love died too, committing suicide at his grave. The two reportedly doomed to aimlessly search for each other throughout eternity.

**A Final Note**

Several years after I published this blog I received an email from a woman who brought me back to reality. I hope it brings some others back as well:

*"One of your post about the Chinese Graveyard in San Antonio, Tx has pictures of my brothers grave. Let it be known that this cemetery is not haunted nor has it ever been. Please let it be known that it's not haunted, and that every year, that cemetery is destroyed because people believe it is? That on two different occasions a body has been dug up? Or that I have to replace my brother's headstone three times because of ghost haunters? I understand that ghost haunting is fun and exciting but not at the cost of other family members who have to relive death over and over again because people are rude and disrespectful. Thank you."*

# SECTION 6:

# CELEBRITY GRAVES

*"I made my first ever visit to Hollywood Forever [Cemetery, in Hollywood, California] earlier this year. (i've been hanging out in cemeteries since i was a little boy...) i was in L.A. for a week's visit, taking photographs for my … project. anyway, upon first entering HF i recognized something different about the energy there. it was thick and heavy, almost suffocating. i ended up coming back to the cemetery 3 or 4 times that week, one time i just got out of my car and wandered aimlessly amongst the graves and fell to my knees and wept, the energy of love and loss seemed so tangible. unlike i've ever felt it in any other cemetery elsewhere before."* – Daryl D.

## Charles Bukowski's Grave

Originally published Sunday, August 11, 2013
https://thecemeterytraveler.blogspot.com/2013/08/charles-bukowskis-grave.html

I was in Los Angeles in June of 2013, so of course, I ignored all the Stars Tours, LaBrea Tar Pits, and the Whiskey-a-Go-Go, preferring to visit Charles Bukowski. Well, his grave, that is. I can't say I'm a big fan of his writing, I'm more a fan of his style - which was in the stream-of-consciousness vein, a la Hunter Thompson. I like to do that myself. Bukowski often said "Don't try," and some would think he meant just let the words flow, don't try to make sense of them. His wife, Linda, says it means don't just try, but rather, DO.

"Dirty journalism" is the phrase some people use to describe Bukowski's writing. Some of it borders on pornography (let's just say you wouldn't want to be reading his novel Women on an airplane and have your neighbor glance down at the words). Calling it misogynistic and crude is to put his prose mildly. According to pretty much every Internet source, Bukowski's writing emphasizes the ordinary lives of poor Americans, writing, drinking, relationships with women, and the drudgery of work.

His poetry, however, is quite beautiful. Check out the opening lines from *bang bang*, a poem from his book *Mockingbird Wish Me Luck*: I can't reprint any of it here, unfortunately, as his words are copyrighted.

So what did I expect to find at his grave site? Whatever it was that I was going to find, I suppose. Perhaps liquor bottles and cigarette butts, as I'd read in a few places (Bukowski was a heavy smoker and an alcoholic). In looking it up on the web ahead of time, I saw one reference to "Charles Bukowski's mausoleum," in Green Hills Memorial Park, but that turned out to be misinformation (the World Wide Web is chock full of such things). He is buried in Green Hills – just not in a mausoleum. The memorial park (one of the most beautiful I've ever seen) is in Palos Los Verdes, a suburb of Los Angeles to the south. (Bukowski lived nearby during the last few years of his life, with most of his life spent in L.A.) Being a memorial park, I really didn't expect to see much of anything, except for acres of flush-to-the-ground grave markers. Such places seldom have statues and are not of the Victorian era, so they've never held much interest for me. Green Hills, though, was a bit different.

Driving through the expensive-looking driveway past the flower store to the guard's booth, it was obvious that this place caters to the well-to-do (which I don't believe "Hank" was, so I'm not sure why he's here). Perfectly manicured lawns and rolling hills with gazebos, statues, and other memorials set Green Hills apart from any memorial park I'd ever seen. It was truly serene and respectful, with all the ambiance of a traditional cemetery. The memorial park, a relatively modern development in cemetery design (the first being California's Forest Lawn in 1912), is usually a flat field that allows the grass to be cut with great ease – totally blasé. The sheer quantity of giant shade trees in Green Hills would seem to impose the traditional challenges in cemetery lawn care.

Bukowski's granite grave marker is just like the thousands of others at Green Hills: rectangular, flat, and flush-to-the-ground. So how did I find it? You can get some general directions off the Internet ("Oceanview" section of the memorial park), but not for the specific location of his grave. (These days people sometimes post GPS coordinates of graves which allows for great ease in locating.) I asked the guard at the entrance booth. Actually there were two gentlemen, both of whom were very helpful. Still, I had difficulty finding it amongst a hundred or so graves in "Oceanview." The name, by the way, is kind of a misnomer - although his grave on the hillside does indeed face the Pacific Ocean, there is a mountain range in the way. The ocean is a couple of miles from here. You can't actually "view" it.

Wandering around the section photographing the grave markers here and there, I was struck by the individuality in the designs. I've never seen that anywhere else. Most of the plates were metal, and were embossed with waterfalls, trees, and other bucolic scenes. Some even had short epitaphs. Finally, a grounds keeper came up the road in a little cart and I flagged him down. He knew Bukowski's marker was around here somewhere, and we walked around a bit without finding it. Then, another worker came up the road in a pickup truck. The first groundskeeper flagged him down and asked if he know where Bukowsi's marker was. The fellow in the pickup replied, "The writer?"

Which reminds me of a blonde joke (but this really happened):
I was at work back around 2002 when two saleswomen came in to the department. One of my coworkers sat at a workbench just outside my office. I heard people talking so I went out to see who was there. One woman was blonde, the other brunette. The brunette pointed to my coworker and said to the blonde, "Doesn't he remind you of Ernest Hemingway?" The blonde said, "The writer?" There's a reason stereotypes exist.

Anyway, the first groundskeeper kept up the search ("Don't Try" - *do*!) and eventually found Bukowski's grave marker for me. "Hank's"' grave was devoid of whiskey bottles and beer cans, so I assume such litter is not a regular occurrence, otherwise the groundskeepers would've known exactly where the grave was. I did pick up a pine cone, however, from beneath a nearby tree. (The name "Hank" on the grave marker is short for Henry Charles "Hank" Chinaski, Bukowski's literary alter ego, a character who appeared many time in Bukowski's books). The 1987 movie, Barfly, was actually based on Chinaski's fictitious life and times.

In 1986, Time magazine called Bukowski the "laureate of American lowlife." After visiting his grave, I celebrated this by stopping for beer and ribs under a tent in a nearby Pep Boys parking lot. As I was eating dinner out of a Styrofoam container in my rental car I started thinking bizarre thoughts. You cannot help but think them when you're contemplating Bukowski – dive bars in L.A., alcoholism, mortality and death - all in the warm California sun.

Here's what I thought of: writing about the connections I have to famous people, no matter how many times removed. Charles Bukowski spent seventeen days in Philadelphia's Moyamensing Prison in 1944 on suspicion of draft evasion. My connection? I lived, at the time, on Moyamensing Avenue, a few blocks from where the prison once stood here in South Philadelphia (it was torn down in 1968). There's an ACME supermarket there now, and I shop in it. Another, somewhat more famous writer, Edgar Allen Poe, also spent some time here (the prison, not the ACME) for public drunkenness in 1849.

Photograph by Chris Snyder

## Eddie Lang – Father of Jazz Guitar

Originally published Tuesday, March 5, 2013
https://thecemeterytraveler.blogspot.com/2013/03/eddie-lang-jazz-guitar-great.html

I'd seen this monument in Holy Cross Cemetery (Yeadon, Pennsylvania) off and on for the fifteen years I'd been making photographs in cemeteries (I lived near Yeadon, which is just outside Philadelphia). I never paid much attention to it, which is odd, because I play guitar. I often see the likenesses of musical instruments engraved on the headstones of the musicians buried beneath, but since from a distance, the name "Massaro" did not jump out at me as being anyone famous, I paid little attention.

## Where Dead Voices Gather

After recently reading the appropriately titled book, *Where Dead Voices Gather* (2001, Little, Brown and Company), by Nick Tosches, I learned that Salvatore Massaro was the real name of jazz guitar legend Eddie Lang. Now, I realize that Eddie Lang is not a familiar name to most people, but please bear with. Lang was predominantly a session musician and frequently played in orchestras back in the 1920s when the music recording industry was still in its infancy. He played on the records of Bessie Smith, Louis Armstrong, Bing Crosby, and other well-known artists. (Crosby, by the way, after having worked with Lang in 1931, insisted that Lang accompany him on all his recordings and performances. He would have no other guitarist.)

We think of guitar players as flamboyant front-and-center rock stars who typically share the stage with an even more flamboyant lead singer in a rock band. Wasn't always that way – in fact, the idea of a specific band of musicians writing and performing its own music in public didn't exist until Buddy Holly created it in 1955. The protypical three-piece rock band with voice, guitar, bass, and drums was created by Holly. Prior to that, musicians were interchangeable, just part of the band, or the orchestra. The stars of the performance were the band leaders, for example, Tommy and Jimmy Dorsey, Duke Ellington, Benny Goodman, etc. The majority of people who actually played the music were faceless, interchangeable, and essentially anonymous to the music-listening public. Even the lead singers were just part of the band. Eddie Lang spent most of his short career as one of these 'background' musicians.

Along with Lonnie Johnson, Lang was a true pioneer of the guitar, playing mostly studio jazz sessions for other people in the early days of recorded music (1920s onward). In fact, his recorded duets with Johnson are considered to be the first important interracial partnership in jazz. Possibly due to the expected adverse reaction by the public to a black man and a white man working as equals, Lang's – or rather, Massaro's name appeared as "Blind Willie Dunn" on the recordings with Lonnie Johnson! (Listen to one of their duets, "Guitar Blues," on your favorite internet music site.)

Eddie Lang, a South Philly native, played an acoustic archtop guitar, which you can see in the plaque on his grave marker (he's holding a Gibson L-5 model). This type guitar had a bigger sound for live playing – a regular acoustic guitar could easily be drowned out by other instruments. Electrical amplification of the guitar was not to be invented until 1934, a year after Lang's death. Charlie Christian was a later guitar pioneer from the jazz era, who played such an electrically-amplified guitar. However, neither Christian nor Lang achieved anywhere near the guitar-god status of their disciple, Django Reinhardt. Reinhardt is much more widely known, having achieved worldwide fame a bit later, in the 1940s, as part of the Parisian musical jazz combo known as the Quintette du Hot Club de France. At least as famous as Django's "hot" jazz guitar playing technique was his pairing with the gypsy violin virtuoso Stephane Grappelli.

A lot goes on with musical recycling. Nowadays everything is derivative. One musician borrows another's riff, a rapper samples an old-school rock song, melodies and styles of playing are copied. True originals are rare. Lang was one of the rare people, the innovators. The guitar was simply not used as he used it – he created a percussive-style playing with occasional lead fills, as well as melodic instrumentals (check out his piece, "April Kisses," on your favorite internet music site). Not only was his style of playing novel, but his guitar-based interpretations of popular songs helped pave the way for public acceptance of the guitar as a serious instrument (believe it or not, the public much preferred to hear banjo at the time!). Andres Segovia did the same for the classical guitar, in his interpretations of classical music written generations before him for other, more "serious," instruments. Segovia, coincidentally, was the only extant guitarist that Lang held in any esteem.

Lang altered the course of music in several ways. Remember I mentioned Django's Quintette du Hot Club de France? The band's main attraction was the dueling interplay between Django's guitar and Grappelli's wild gypsy violin. So here's an interesting bit of trivia: Eddie Lang actually originated the idea of the jazz guitar and violin combo with his boyhood friend Joe Venuti. They recorded together as the Joe Venuti-Eddie Lang Blue Five. (Check out one of their compositions, "Four String Joe," recorded in 1927.) After Lang's death in 1933, Venuti went on to become the first jazz master of the violin, and Django and Grappelli formed the Hot Club of France. Eddie Lang, i.e. Salvatore Massaro, died in 1933, due to bleeding complications following a routine tonsillectomy.

Yes, the world lost Eddie Lang at the ripe young age of thirty-one! All because Bing Crosby talked him into getting a tonsillectomy – Crosby thought this would improve Lang's singing voice. Yes, the mortal world lost him, but the world of music is all the richer because of his virtuosic talents. This is evidenced by the thousands of recordings he made both as a solo artist, an accompanist, and an orchestra player. You can see him performing with Joe Venuti in the 1930 film, "King of Jazz."

## Epilogue

Some time after I posted the essay above, Eddie Lang's nephew contacted me. He lives in the Philadelphia area. Mr. Massaro was quite appreciative of the blog and told me he has been working for years to bring to the public's attention his uncle's contribution to American music. "The

Father of Jazz Guitar" is a majestic enough title (and well-deserved), but rock and roll fans should realize this about Eddie Lang: if not for him, the banjo would still be the stringed instrument of choice in American popular music! Lang single-handedly changed America's – and the world's – perception of the guitar as a publicly-acceptable musical instrument! If not for Lang, a.k.a. Salvatore Massaro, there would never have been a Clapton, Page, or Hendrix. Imagine what the 1980s hair band hit, "Livin' on a Prayer," would have sounded like, played by *Ban* Jovi instead of Bon Jovi!

# Nancy Spungen's Flattened Tombstone

Originally published Thursday, May 26, 2011
https://thecemeterytraveler.blogspot.com/2011/05/flattened-tombstones.html

What do Nancy Spungen (of "Sid and Nancy" fame) and actor John Barrymore have in common? Admittedly, not much. However, they both have flat-to-the-ground tombstones. Spungen is buried in a cemetery where flat stones are required, and Barrymore, along with the rest of the Barrymore theatrical dynasty, seems to have chosen flat markers by choice. While practical, I can't imagine anything more mundane. Which is odd, since both were larger-than-life characters.

Back in the early 1990s, I made a trip to Forest Lawn Cemetery in Glendale California to see the Lone Ranger's grave, among others. I found that the majority of the 250,000 inhabitants have flush to the ground grave markers - all the same size! I certainly didn't find it very attractive - grassy fields punctuated with cheesy modern sculptures here and there. I could find none of the graves I came there to see. I remember asking the groundskeeper why it is like this, and he replied, beaming, "It makes it so easy to cut the grass!"

Obviously, that's the main attraction – ease of maintenance. But I just don't get it. Granted, we could not reproduce the splendor of a Victorian sculpture garden cemetery today - the cost would be prohibitive. Plus, stone carving just ain't what it used to be! While garden cemeteries had a distinct plan, the sheer variety of the monuments themselves gave an air of and uniqueness to each cemetery.

The trend today, of course, is vastly different. Flat markers, or "grass markers," as they are sometimes called, are only one of many regulations we are sometimes warned about. Cemeteries typically have rules concerning the size and type of headstone, marker, or memorial. For example, Catholic cemeteries might require a religious design on the headstone. Many cemeteries forbid personal, whimsical ornamentation like pinwheels or solar-powered lights.

As it turns out, the Forest Lawn Cemetery chain (in Southern California) may have actually been the instigator of the trend toward flat grave markers. In 1906, Forest Lawn was founded by a group of San Francisco businessmen, with Dr. Hubert Eaton credited as its founder. According to Wikipedia, Eaton developed the "memorial park plan," of eliminating upright grave markers. He felt that the upright grave markers were an eyesore, and ruined the aesthetic of the park-like idea of a cemetery. He did not want to provide visitors with more overt reminders of death; he preferred trees, fountains, and clean-cut lawns on rolling hillsides. So in a cemetery filled with flat markers, how do visitors even find the graves of their loved ones? If the grounds are not maintained, grass and dirt can just cover them up! And what about all the states where it snows? I can see Forest Lawn not needing to concern itself with this, but the Barrymore and Spungen graves are in the Northeast part of the U.S. – Pennsylvania, in fact. It snows here! And what about Jack Kerouac's flat stone in Lowell, Massachusetts? Do you just not go and visit your loved ones' graves in the winter? I thought about this the first time I visited King David Memorial Park, in Bensalem, Pennsylvania, where Nancy Spungen is buried.

Granted, my trip to Glendale was in the early 1990s, and the Internet was not yet the wealth of information that it is today. Websites like FindAGrave.com now help us in our quest to locate specific graves. During a current search for comedian Sam Kinison's burial place, I was surprised to find such specific directions for his grave site in Memorial Park Cemetery, Tulsa, Oklahoma. Plot, section name and number are available along with GPS coordinates N 36°05.095 W 095°52.814.

I think I'll end my little rant here with a story about Spungen's grave, and how Sid Vicious' mom wanted to bury his ashes there. The punk rock musician from the Sex Pistols supposedly stabbed his girlfriend Nancy to death in their suite at the Chelsea Hotel in Manhattan in 1978. Spungen was laid to rest at King David Memorial Park (a northeastern suburb of Philadelphia), in Bucks county, PA. Vicious was arrested for the murder, but never went to trial. Three months later while out on bail, he overdosed on heroin and died. His mom, Ann, and some close friends had Sid's body cremated and intended to fulfill Sid's wish: "When I die, bury me next to Nancy."

Spungen's mother, however, wanted no part of such a thing, so the keepers of Sid's ashes attempted to do what my family has done in the past – illegally bury them on another person's plot. As bizarre as the account is, I can relate. Eileen Polk describes the experience in the book, *Please Kill Me, The Uncensored Oral History of Punk*; Polk was a photographer and friend of Sid and Nancy.

She and Sid's mother, Ann, drove to Philadelphia with Sid's ashes, hoping to lay them to rest on Nancy's grave. The grounds were snow-covered at the time. Some workers from King David Memorial Park showed them to Nancy's grave, but would not leave. The visitors could not very well tell the attendants what they proposed to do, as there are rules against that. Not the least of which is the prohibition of burying non-Jews in a Jewish burial ground (Nancy was Jewish, Sid was not). So the visitors paid their respects and drove out of the cemetery. They parked their car nearby. Sid's mother took the can of ashes, climbed the fence, went back to Nancy's grave, and dumped his ashes out. Sid and Nancy were finally together, sort of, their odyssey over.

# Live Video Streaming from Andy Warhol's Grave

Originally published Thursday, August 6, 2015
https://thecemeterytraveler.blogspot.com/2015/08/live-video-streaming-from-andy-warhols.html

Andy Warhol has a hard time staying dead. In fact, it has been almost thirty years since he passed on (in 1987) to that great celeb party in the sky. Warhol is even more popular now than he was when he walked the earth with his tape recorder and Polaroid camera. These days, he is certainly more widely known and appreciated. His art is fabulous, of course, but it his IDEAS that continue to inspire. Such is the case with the "Figment" project.

I assume some cemeteries have video surveillance for security reasons. St. John the Baptist Byzantine Catholic Cemetery in the Bethel Park neighborhood of Pittsburgh's south hills has it for another reason – to create art. And if you visit, you can easily get your fifteen minutes of fame, as Warhol once quipped about the future.

Two years ago today, on August 6, 2013 (in honor of Andy's birthday), The Warhol Museum in Pittsburgh in conjunction with EarthCam, launched a collaborative project called "Figment," a live feed of Andy's gravesite.

The feed can be viewed at this link:

https://www.earthcam.com/usa/pennsylvania/pittsburgh/warhol/index.php?cam=warhol_figmentstream

Why "Figment?" Well, Warhol had said that he'd I'd like his own headstone to be blank. No epitaph, no name, well, actually, he said, I'd like it to say 'figment.' (https://www.warhol.org/andy-warhols-life/figment/)
Rubbing of Andy Warhol's headstone

Andy's headstone is in fact not blank, as you can see in this photograph I made in the cemetery during my visit on July 22, 2015. And speaking of the inscription – and this is kind of a bizarre coincidence – I purchased a framed rubbing of his headstone engraving at a thrift shop a few years ago. I knew it was authentic, as I had visited Warhol's grave site back in 2000, and recognized the design.

**The Grave Site**

St. John the Baptist Byzantine Catholic Cemetery is in a blue collar neighborhood, a smallish cemetery on a pronounced hillside. The headstones are plain, the statuary meager. I could not remember where Warhol's grave was, since it been many years since my last visit. On driving up the hill past the gatehouse and the BVM adorned with a spray of fresh flowers, I instantly saw the utility pole with two video cameras mounted to it. Ah, simply follow the line of sight and I should find the grave. There is was, Campbell's Tomato Soup cans and all, about a hundred feet from the pole.

There are two video cameras (says the live Internet link) so one can provide the long view of the grave site and the other a zoomed-in view. You may notice the larger "Warhola" family grave marker behind Andy's if you watch the EarthCam live feed. His parents Andrew and Julia are buried there behind him; Warhola was Andy's real last name (he dropped the final "a"). Besides live video, an interesting thing about the EarthCam website is that periodically, webcam still images are posted in the archive for everyone's enjoyment! As you can imagine, some odd things are bound to happen here from time to time. The images are labeled with time and date. Another interesting thing, to me, anyway, is that in 2012, Madalen Warhola, Andy's niece, purchased a photograph I made of a cemetery angel. I was involved in a group art exhibition entitled "Warholized." Your entry had to be in some way influenced by Warhol's art. Madalen was one of the judges, the other was Andy's nephew, James Warhola. The angel she purchased may have reminded her that Uncle Andy's career was launched by his artistic renderings of cherubs for various advertising campaigns.

See my blog post, "Warholized Cemetery Angels," for more of that story:
https://thecemeterytraveler.blogspot.com/2012/02/warholized-cemetery-angels.html

A few days after my visit, I checked the time I was present at the grave site on the video archive – July 22, 2015 (2 pm) – to see if there were any images of me hanging a found rosary around the Coca-Cola bottle at the top of Andy's headstone. (You can see the rosary in the photo above; Andy was quite religious, believe it or not!) Alas, my visit apparently was not as noteworthy as some others (e.g. birthday parties for Andy, typically the weekend around his actual birthday, August the sixth!), for I am not archived in the EarthCam Hall of Fame. We do see recent images of, for instance, a bunny visiting the gravesite, as well as an Elvis impersonator. I can see how Elvis could easily have been chosen over me, but … a rabbit? Perhaps Andy implied that every creature will have its fifteen minutes of fame … I did notice in scenes after my visit that someone moved my rosary from the Coke bottle to one of the Campbell's soup cans – maybe it was the Elvis impersonator. I like to think that I helped create new Pop Art.

There is also a plastic file folder in front of Warhol's headstone in which you can write a note to Andy. This is part of artist Madelyn Roehrig's ongoing art project "Figments: Conversations with Andy" (https://www.facebook.com/conversationswithandy). Roehrig publishes them on the Facebook site "Conversations With Andy" (https://www.facebook.com/conversationswithandy). I would highly recommend checking this page a few times around Andy's birthday – August 6 – to see what sort of craziness Andy's fans may be up to. The EarthCam site should also be vibrant with ceremony – as Andy said, art is what you can get away with!

So if you are interested in your own your fifteen minutes of fame, consider a visit to Warhol's grave in St. John the Baptist Byzantine Catholic Cemetery in Pittsburgh, Pennsylvania's Bethel Park neighborhood. And don't forget the Warhol Museum in downtown Pittsburgh!

# "On the Road" with Jack Kerouac

Originally published Saturday, September 18, 2010
https://thecemeterytraveler.blogspot.com/2010/09/on-road-with-jack-kerouac-and-cemetery.html

It is fitting that The Cemetery Traveler would visit the grave of Jack Kerouac, pop culture's most famous traveler. I was driving through New England a few years back and made it a point to stop to see his grave, at the Edson City Cemetery in Lowell, Massachusetts.

Known mainly for his 1957 epic travel adventure novel, *On the Road*, Kerouac epitomized wanderlust for an entire generation. He continues to do so now, years after his death. You simply cannot read *On the Road* without wanting to just drive recklessly off into the sunset in search of Meaning. I read it, and bought a convertible.

So why would I want to visit his grave? Why would anyone want to visit a celebrity's grave? Some of us do this because it enables us to get closer to the person than we could possibly have gotten in real life – a brush with greatness, as it were. For me, I think it was to get closer to the spirit of Kerouac's writing (which has a maddening stream-of-consciousness style further popularized a decade later by Hunter S. Thompson in his book, Fear and Loathing in Las Vegas). Kerouac isn't exactly a role model for me, its just that his writing touched a nerve. I've kind of always felt, as Kerouac did, that a pearl would be handed to me at some point. But really, for that to happen, one must be willing to leap, with the expectation that the net will appear (as American naturalist John Burroughs so eloquently stated).

I think I was driving back from a ski trip in New Hampshire, when I decided to stop in Lowell. Lowell is a mill town, and was America's textile epicenter during the Industrial Revolution. A workingman's town, and Kerouac's hometown. He was born there in 1922 – Jean-Louis Lebris de Kerouac. He was French-Canadian, his parents had immigrated from Quebec, Canada. You'll notice the stone says "Jean," not Jack.

Edson City Cemetery is a relatively large, yet flat and plain looking property. The woman at the gatehouse is happily prepared to give you a map showing how to get to the grave (it is arguably Lowell's most popular tourist attraction). Otherwise it would be rather difficult to find as Kerouac's grave marker is flush with the ground. Let me rephrase that – its actually easy to find if you just take note of the several cars lined up waiting near the grave. This was the oddest thing! No one would bother you as you paid your respects, lit your candle, or left your token offering. As you drove away, the next car would drive up almost religiously, people would get out, walk to the grave, and spend some quiet moments. What were they reflecting on, I wondered? And why such reverence? I've never witnessed such a spectacle.

I've visited the grave sites of dozens of celebrities (in their own right) and have never encountered another live visitor. Not that I really expected anyone to be hanging out near mathematician Kurt Godel's grave in Princeton (yeah, I'm a fan), but wouldn't you expect to see at least a few people at Rudolph Valentino's grave in Hollywood? Or Marilyn Monroe's? I mean, even given the fact that the Hollywood Grave Line Tours will not allow people to get out and walk around ...

So these people still line up to visit Kerouac's grave, decades after his death. Why? Are they, like On the Road characters Sal and Dean, actually on a spiritual quest? Why such reverence? Kerouac's friend Jim Holmes said that the real journey of Kerouac's characters was inward, having adventures along the way as they searched for a belief on the other side.

Maybe that's part of the reason I tear off at the drop of a hat – in my convertible – in search of new cemeteries to photograph. The creative process of photography has always helped me deal with the world, with personal issues, and even to judge myself (in retrospect, psychiatry would've been cheaper). However, I believe that spending time in cemeteries has helped me search for, and sometimes find, meaning in an otherwise entropic world. Seeing others find meaning in my work is an unexpected gift.

# Elizabeth Barrett Browning

https://thecemeterytraveler.blogspot.com/2010/07/gypsies-in-english-cemetery.html
Originally published Friday, July 2, 2010, as *Gypsies in the English Cemetery*

In 2008, I visited The English Cemetery (also known as the Protestant Cemetery) in Florence Italy. My wife and I had just seen Michelangelo's David at the Accademia and decided to spend a few hours on individual missions. Mine was to continue walking about a half mile to the Piazzalle Donatello, site of the only cemetery in Florence.

The only traditionally Victorian cemetery, that is. Since these tend to have more statuary and other ornamentation than do the catacombs, I wanted to see it. Ancient, stately cities in Italy like Florence and Rome have above-ground outdoor Victorian cemeteries, but most of the cities' dead are buried in catacombs. The name "Victorian," by the way, implies that the cemetery was designed during the era 1837 - 1901 (the reign of Britain's

Queen Victoria). Owned by the Swiss and managed by the English, the English Cemetery originated as an ecumenical burial spot for non-Catholics and non-Jews (who were previously not allowed burial in the city of Florence).

On approaching the grounds, I noted with dismay that the gates were locked. As I tried to figure out how to get in, I noticed a woman in a light blue nun's habit scurrying around the cemetery buildings. I headed over to talk with her and she was most gracious – even though the cemetery was closed, she let me in to photograph the statuary. I spent about an hour amidst the magnificent sculpture (American sculpture can hardly hold a candle to Italian craftsmanship), amazed that there was no graffiti, vandalism, or damage from acid rain. I asked the nun at that point if she could please direct me to Elizabeth Barrett Browning's grave.

The nun – who turned out to be the accomplished author Julia Bolton Holloway, PhD – was a most amazing host! Caretaker of the English Cemetery, Julia is from Britain (her PhD is in Medieval Studies). She retired from academics as Professor Emerita to join an Anglican convent. She explained to me the history of the cemetery, as well as its curious upkeep. It seems that Julia routinely affords sanctuary to gypsies traveling west from Romania (it is illegal for them to be in Florence). She educates their children, while in return, the adults spend a few weeks restoring rusted ironwork and rebuilding stone walls and monuments. She marvels at their abilities and explains that this is the predominant method of restoration here.

Julia took me to where Browning's monument stood. Her grave marker (essentially a catafalque, a raised platform supporting the coffin) is rather large – possibly the largest in the cemetery. I was of course embarrassed that I'd walked right past it – several times! Afterward, Julia offered to show me the "historic" photographs. We went into the gatehouse, through a library where four or five monks pored over architectural drawings of the cemetery, then into a darkened room with framed photographs on the walls. Each piece had a small curtain over it to protect it from light degradation. You had to pull the material aside to see the image. All were original black and white images of the cemetery, made in the late 1800s. On the way out through the library, I noticed all the childrens' crayon drawings on the walls. I asked her why some of the gypsy children's artwork involved helicopters. She told me that police raids and arrests by helicopter are a common occurrence among the gypsies.

I also noted a small stack of copies of the book, "Aurora Leigh and Other Poems of Elizabeth Barrett Browning." I mentioned that it seemed like a good idea to sell copies of such things here to raise money for the cemetery. Julia modestly stated that she was the editor of the text! I purchased a copy and asked her to autograph it for me, which she did. As a fitting end to my visit to the English Cemetery, my proper British host called me a cab on her cell phone and bade me good day.

# SECTION 7:

# GETTING PERSONAL

My Artist's Statement, when I participate in public hangings (of my photography, that is):

*"Simply put, my work merges art and photography with society's desire to come to terms with death and dying."*

With the addition of *The Cemetery Traveler* blog, my work now merges words with all that other stuff.

++++++++++++++++

*"Interesting how when you hear someone say they've written about the death of a relative, one (or I) instantly think, 'oh it will be sentimental and relevant to the person who wrote it and I'll be polite', clearly not the case here. That was just great Ed. you do have quite an interesting history!"* – Carol F.

*"Wow, quite a story and entertainingly told. I would never have guessed at the infamy of your family, you seem like such an upstanding fellow. then again, there is that whole cemetery thing."* – Valerie K.

# Nana's Ashes

Originally published Friday, December 17, 2010
https://thecemeterytraveler.blogspot.com/2010/12/nanas-ashes.html

A number of secrets were buried with my Lithuanian grandmother, Leona Snyder, in 2000. She spent the last five of her ninety-two years in a nursing home, the final two years suffering with dementia. Late in the game, she made hardly any sense—to me, anyway. She would be very loving toward my children one minute, then not remember their names the next. It was heartbreaking to see her degradation from the six-foot matriarchal battleaxe and stalwart of our highly dysfunctional family. That's her at left in the photo above with a grandchild on her knee. That's me third from the right, looking right at you (maybe I'm eight?). The noose, I'm afraid, defies explanation.

Once while visiting her, her youngest sister (then in her sixties) was present. "Nana," as we called my grandmother, went off on some unintelligible tangent about their sister not leaving them a penny when she died, having accumulated "a chain of whorehouses that the state got hold of." Both her sister and I nodded in agreement until Nana fell asleep. Out in the hallway, I lamented to my great aunt about how difficult it is for me to see my grandmother this way, just rambling incoherently. She said, "What do you mean? You didn't know about any of that?" Their heretofore unmentioned entrepreneurial sister actually ran a business that serviced Northeast Pennsylvania coal miners in the early 1900s! I have every reason to believe that Nana is living as colorful an afterlife as she did a physical life.

When she died, it was decided to bury her ashes at her parents' gravesite. My family has cremated most of its kin, for reasons of economy, they've said. In retrospect and since they all hated funerals as much as I do, I suspect the real reason is because they cannot bear to see their relation in a coffin surrounded by flowers. Many folks just don't like long goodbyes. Seeing their loved one die gave them all the sense of closure they needed. Disposal of the body was a simple housekeeping task.

I don't even know where the cremation was done (some details we just block out, you know?). I do remember, however, my parents asking me to bury the ashes. My first thought was to do this in some romantic fashion, such as scattering them across several farmers' fields where she had us, as children, steal corn. She'd pull the car over to the side of the road and throw a bag at us: "Fill this up—they'll never miss it!" However, the family thought it fitting to bury her ashes at her parents' grave. Now this isn't as "normal" as it may sound. Her parents' grave stone had originally been stolen by her two brothers – a nice large granite model lifted from a monument dealer's outdoor display. They took it to some other stone carver to have it engraved.

The intent, on my part, was to not notify the owners of that little rural cemetery that we were burying her ashes here. While its okay to scatter someone's cremains to the four winds, you're not supposed to just dig a hole on someone's private property and bury them! One could argue that we already owned the plot, right, so we should be able to do whatever we want on it, right? Well, cemeteries make their money by selling you a burial plot, charging you to dig the hole, engraving the stone, providing you with a memorial service, and perhaps, a fancy urn for the cremains. That's how they stay in business. Nothing wrong with any of that.

Doing stuff illegally just runs in my family's blood, I guess. As much as I enjoyed them, many were either criminals, liars, or drunks, and sometimes all three – actual descendants of Molly Maguires gone awry. I should point out that this would be on my father's side. Once when paying a surprise visit to Nana's brother, "Uncle Joe," in Maryland, we found his house burned and boarded up. At about fourteen, I remember walking into the Glen Burnie police station with Nana as she went up to the officer at the front desk and said (and I'm sure she had no inkling of his actual rank), "Sergeant, we're looking for Joseph Wilkes." Without even looking up from his paperwork, he replied, "Who isn't, lady?" We slunk out of there.

So one Spring day, three carloads of us drove to the hillside cemetery out in the boonies of NEPA (Northeastern Pennsylvania) where Nana's parents are buried. Not much going on, it being a weekend and the quarry down the road was closed. No houses for a quarter mile in any direction. We were all uncomfortably polite to each other—my parents, an aunt with her daughter and child, my brother, and my cousin Albert. You know how you begin to feel twelve years old again after spending a half-hour with your parents? Not this time; I was 42 years old and felt strangely adult. Nana was there too—her ashes, that is, in a plastic bag.

Albert and I found ourselves in front of the stolen family headstone, shovel in hand. Time settles down and concentrates on the moment, as writer Salman Rushdie would say. Albert and I hadn't seen each other in twenty years, but we had been almost inseparable as kids. We shared many formative experiences (e.g. crawling under the fence of the washed-out Forty-Fort Cemetery mentioned at the beginning of this book) – mainly during weekends and summers spent at Nana's. I dug an adequate hole and Albert and I opened the bag. Over some nervously light banter, we began pouring the ashes into the hole. As the wind began to kick up and ashes took flight, I looked at him and asked with a grin, "You ever see 'The Big Lebowski?," thinking of the scene where John Goodman empties a coffee can of Donny's ashes off a Pacific coast cliff and the wind blows them into Jeff Bridges' face. Albert snickered and said, "Yeah…"

No member of my family ever won an award for subtlety. Remember "The Loud Family" from the late 1970's seasons of Saturday Night Live? Where everybody yelled? You know my people then. You could never be certain what they said was true, but they more than made up for that in sheer volume. That said, as our little caravan of cars left the cemetery, my cousin Albert pulled an M-80 (about equal to 1/20 stick of dynamite) out of his shirt pocket, lit it, and threw it out the car window! WTF! As the goddamn thing exploded in the woods, we heard invisible horses frantically neighing, as if someone had just uttered "FRAU BLUCHER!" (you know, in Mel Brooks' movie Young Frankenstein…?). When the main road behind the quarry came into view, we saw two horses reared up on their hind legs with their riders – still mounted – clutching their reins for dear life! As the horses with their helpless riders galloped down the dirt road like twin bats out of hell, I realized that grieving is a very individual thing—and Albert was grieving in his own special way. It was the perfect denouement to my grandmother's complex and overbearing life, a fitting tribute.

# Graves of Lost Siblings

Originally published Friday, July 27, 2012
https://thecemeterytraveler.blogspot.com/2012/07/graves-of-lost-siblings.html

In a couple weeks I'm planning a trip, the trip of a lifetime. A few years ago, my Mom let it be known that she was in fact, not an only child. She had two brothers and a sister. They were all born seven to ten years after her, and all died shortly after birth. My Mom also let it be known that they were buried in a cemetery in Shavertown, Pennsylvania (near where she lives in northeast PA), the vicinity in which I was born and raised. I've asked her to take me there, to see the graves. I'm writing this before the fact. I'm not at all sure what I'm in for. So keep your hat on, we may end up miles from here.

Since my Dad died eight years ago, my Mom has been talking. This may seem unusual. However, my Dad was overbearing to the point where he monopolized all conversations and didn't allow other people to speak – and this was one of his better qualities. Our lives basically revolved around his family. My Mom's family was seldom mentioned, and never visited – the living or dead.

So after he died, my Mom started to talk. It's been great. I've learned wonderful things about her family – my family. The most shocking thing was the existence of Robert Daniel, Daniel Robert, and Joyce Elizabeth – and the fact that she knew where they were buried.

I didn't know any of this back in 1981 when my first wife was pregnant with our first child. It died in utero and had to be aborted. My mother, after the fact, wanted to have a tree planted in the baby's memory in a local park. Both my ex-wife and I thought that was ludicrous. We just wanted to forget the horrific experience. About twenty years later, my mother told me that she had gone ahead anyway and had that tree planted. I figured, whatever, if it means that much to you, fine. I forgot about that tree until she began telling me about her lost siblings.

I realized in a flash how meaningful it was to her to plant that tree. She needed something like that to hold on to the memory of what, at the time, could have been her first and maybe only grandchild. People cherish things they've lost in all sorts of ways, and far be it for me to criticize any of them. We all need tangible links to our past. Over the past thirty years I've provided my mom with four wonderful grandchildren, all of whom she loves and adores. Perhaps even more than she would have if she had not lost the first.

So the fateful day arrived when we planned to visit the cemetery where her siblings are buried. We did this yesterday – my Mom, my brother Tim, and I. After literally months of ninety-degree weather and near-drought conditions in this part of the country, this is the day it rained like hell. I made the wet, hundred mile drive to Wilkes-Barre, Pennsylvania, the general area in which my Mom lives. We all jumped into my brother's car and drove out to Shavertown, where Evergreen Cemetery is located. I lived around here for the first nineteen years of my life and never knew this cemetery existed.

My mom, it turned out, had not been to Evergreen since 1945, when her newborn sister Joyce Elizabeth died, and was buried here. She surprised herself by remembering approximately where the plots were, but we had to search a bit for the actual grave markers. First we found the Jones plot, in which are buried her grandparents, Daniel and Elizabeth Jones. Seeing my mom standing on her grandparents' graves and looking teary was heartbreaking, as she said that my deceased father had not allowed her to visit these graves. I felt the weight of that history. Daniel and Elizabeth had a son, Daniel Jr. (who is not buried here), who became my mom's father. Daniel Sr. died in 1920 and Elizabeth later remarried Robert Berwick, whose family plot is about fifty feet away. My mom's siblings are all buried at the larger Berwick plot.

Until I saw the headstones, I thought it unusual (or even uncreative) to name your first-born boys Robert Daniel and Daniel Robert. But seeing the names engraved on the stones explained all: Daniel was the children's (including my mom) biological grandfather and Robert was their step-grandfather. (My birth certificate middle name, by the way, is Daniel.) As I said, I always thought my mom was an only child. Her parents Daniel Jr. and wife Anna tried to have more children after my mom was born (in 1938), but the children did not live. Daniel Robert contracted pneumonia and died shortly after birth. Robert Daniel was born with his umbilical cord wrapped around his neck and died at birth. (My son Christopher was also born with the cord wrapped around his neck, but as the delivery took place in a tertiary care medical center in 1990, he received better medical care and survived.)

My mom was six or eight years old when her brothers were born (and died) and does not remember much about the situation. She was ten, however, when her sister Joyce Elizabeth was born. She remembers the baby had a dislocated hip, among other problems, and died shortly after birth. Although the boys were buried at the Berwick family plot, she was not present at the burial. She does remember, however, being present at Joyce Elizabeth's burial. She said "I remember them lowering that little white casket into the ground." I just about broke down when she said that.

Standing on their graves sixty-seven years later, she added, "They were all beautiful babies. I wonder what they would have looked like if they lived." I suggested, "Like you?" She smirked and said, "What, short and fat?" None of the children's names appear on the Berwick stone, for whatever reason. A gigantic evergreen shades the plot. As I was standing beneath it with my family, feeling firmly present in my past, I thought about that tree my mother had planted for my almost-firstborn. I can't imagine ever being strong enough to visit it though, wherever it is.

## Epilogue

Several years after I posted this blog, I was contacted by a woman from Florida. She told me that the story and photos I posted filled in the lost information in her family tree! Cheryl, it turns out, is my Mom's cousin. They had not seen each other for forty years. She asked if I could please put her in touch with my Mom. Not only was my Mom shocked and elated, but a great new friendship began. Cheryl visited us in Pennsylvania, and we all keep in touch on social media. Cheryl introduced us to my Mom's cousin in Wales, and completed a lovely ancestry picture of my Mom's heritage. My great-grandparents were from North Wales. My great-grandmother was born on a farm called Waen Y Brodlas in Flintshire county, near Flint where my Mom's cousin Dilys lives. During Cheryl's visit, she shocked me by giving me a black and white photograph of myself as a newborn, being held by my great-grandmother, who died before I was a year old. I had never seen a photograph of this woman. So, here's to the power of social media and a beautiful family reunion that would never have occurred without it!

*"What a glorious story, Ed. Tell your mother that I admire her very much. Some gutsy dame! To have carried all that within, and to STILL have a sense of humour. Great stuff. Hey. You go visit that tree ... take your mother's hand ... I suspect she would be one helluva guide."* – Julie S.

## Why do you photograph cemeteries?

Originally published Friday, April 11, 2014
https://thecemeterytraveler.blogspot.com/2014/04/why-do-you-photograph-cemeteries.html

Back in mid-winter (oh, maybe January 2014), I started a Facebook Group Page that I called "Cemeteries in the Snow" (https://www.facebook.com/groups/748427441835492/).
The 2013-14 winter saw snow in 49 of the 50 United States – Florida being the only state in which it did not snow! Due mainly to the exuberant response (there were postings from all over the world – Germany, Canada, Brasil, Great Britain, Poland, even Texas!), it occurred to me to make this post:

*"Ok, here's a question for everyone: Why do you photograph cemeteries?"*

People would ask me this, and for years, I never had a good answer. Sometimes I think about what photographer Annie Leibovitz said when I saw her make a presentation on her photography. She told a story about being a passenger as a child in her family's station wagon, and viewing the world outside through the window frame of the car door. For some of us, there is just this urge to frame and capture moments. This is how we process the world.

Let's take a look at why some people make photographs in cemeteries. I believe I had about 75 responses, almost immediately. I wanted to share some with my Cemetery Traveler readers. You may be surprised by some, amazed at others. In all, they are quite inspiring!

**Denise MacL.** – "As a child, I loved listening to the elderly people telling stories of days gone past...and then I liked to see where these people were buried. After a while, I started visiting cemeteries to read the stones and piece together the history. Then I began to notice the art within and photography became a way for me to capture the beauty found. As well, it fills my 'cup of happiness' to spend a day in such a tranquil place filled with heartwarming 'stories', sentiments and beauty. It is my form of meditation and oddly, I find it exhilarating. I feel more alive after spending the day there."

**Kim P.** – "I began visiting cemeteries with my grandmother when I was a teenager. We mainly went because she shared so much of our family history and visited their graves because these are what remains (seriously no pun intended) of their lives. Their existence is literally written in stone. In the ensuing years as I got older and began soul-searching, I needed to feel as though I belonged in this world, and would visit my ancestors' graves on a regular basis to help me feel grounded. I am not trying to sound cliché by using these words. I mean it very literally. So when digital photography became popular and mainstream, it was just a natural and amazing way for me to carry these images with me. And then I began just visiting cemeteries I encountered wherever I went for the simple peace and beauty of them. I love discovering all the people that have come before me. And I take photos regularly for Find A Grave, and have been able to fill photo requests for people researching their family who do not live near where their ancestors are buried. I derive great joy from "reuniting" family members. It is free and brings me joy and knowledge. I could go on and on, but in a nutshell, that's why I love photographing cemeteries."

**Denise M.** – "It is a passion and an obsession..."

**Alexandra M.** – "My interest in photographing – and writing about – cemeteries developed from my career as a funeral director. I must say that I far prefer spending time in cemeteries in an artistic capacity."

**Dave W.** – "For me it began as a genealogical quest. Placing me in cemeteries, recording the information on tombstones. Then taking photos (35mm) for the addition to my charts. All this bringing me to a large cemetery in the town I grew up in. Thus taking me back to redo the photos with my first Polaroid digital camera. Seeing one of my family plots with the grass over grown, I began to take my mower with me to do these plots. In this process I met the board president of the cemetery, he thanked me, told me the struggles of a non-profit cemetery and since having family in the cemetery I could participate at the board meetings so I went. I continued to take photos of family members in cemeteries, but while in this one I began to see carvings, unique t/stones and began taking more. Sometimes just sitting in the peaceful area and reflecting. Then names of others became interesting. So I starting writing down their histories, which led to a Historical Tour held in October each year, which led to a fundraiser. Placing me in cemeteries more and more, particularly in this one. … So due to the peace of the cemetery, the excitement of a new find, to the beauty of nature and the artistic tombstones, I became, a cemetery junkie! … You did show me the art in it. I like the art, and often place my mind into the chipping and cutting to create. However in my mind it is impossible, lol... Peeling was a local carver here, his forte' was lambs, I just cannot imagine creating such art from stone. Now that is what I look for...... Oh a name once in a while too, but never as before!"

**John O'B.** – "History written in stone."

**Tina DeM.** – "It's a unique canvas of interesting photos and stories waiting to be told."

**Cheryl F.** – "My dad would take me to his family cemeteries in VA when I was a child. He was a photographer and had a darkroom in our basement so I became fascinated with the process. He was more into documentation/genealogy, I was more into the art/landscape in the cemeteries. I began photographing cemetery art when I was in high school and picked it up again when I started teaching pinhole camera design to my sophomore chem students. Now I've published a coffee table book of my cemetery photos so I've really gone over to the darkside LOL."

**Julie E.** – "I started doing it back in the 80's when I was taking photography classes. The teacher was horrified by it. But – it made good black and whites and if I did something I didn't like or didn't get what I wanted I could always go back because those folks — weren't going anywhere. They would always be in the same place – so I could redo till I got what I needed. Unfortunately, I never could have imagined that my life would go the road it did – and I did not save those photos or negatives. I think maybe only two or three photos survive out of hundreds. Imagine the photographic record I would have had for myself in that cemetery. When it came time for me to show [daughter] Megan how to work the manual camera - that's where I took her, to the cemetery."

**Denise J.** – "Because they have a beauty, all their own. Time stands still there."

**Andrea W**. – "Because I love it."

**James V**. – "For some strange reason I've always been attracted to Cemeteries regardless of where I've been. From my hometown in Wisconsin to the one across from my grandmother's house in Colorado. San Diego to Hollywood to Alexandria Virginia. Always respectful always curious. From the statues and artwork to the names and lives they've lived. I personally found photography late in life. Wish I had then. When I finally came up to Philadelphia from VA, the Forest Hills/Shalom was down the street which I ventured. It wasn't until I moved in Mayfair where I found a person who had similar interests in Cemeteries. I found out she was into photography and would photograph cemeteries and certain stones of interest. She showed me Laurel Hill East and West and we would go there taking photos, she with her camera me with my phone, that is until my wonderful wife bought me the best Christmas gift EVER! A D5100 Nikon with 2 lenses. Now I had a real camera, but a lot to learn. As you know, Ed, when we first met at Laurel Hill on photography night was my first night shoots. I've taught myself much since then yet Cemeteries and Tombstones are still my favorite and always will be!

I was up in Easton with a friend, we had spare time and I saw the Easton Cemetery and wanted to stop in and check it out. He was driving and he gave me a look like I was insanely joking and kept driving. I will get up there again one day. … have not had the opportunity to truly investigate it because I'm usually with my family and when I mention stopping in I get the usual uninterested sigh of, 'Omg, no, please don't make us dad.' From my family. Lol"

**Jacqueline T**. – "I've been there [Vandegrift Cemetery, Philadelphia] and shot as much as I could because a lot of the stones are unreadable. It's very small and the people at the fire house across the street were looking at me funny lol...they just wouldn't understand lol..."

**Debra H.** – "I Don't Photograph At All. I Don't Even Own A Camera, Unless You Count The One In My IPad, Or My Old Polaroid- I Don't Even Know Where That Is. Anyway – I Really Am Captivated By This Genre. Even The Post-Mortem Photography Is Interesting To Me. I Very Much Enjoy All Of Your Contributions. Thank You For What You Do!"

**Patricia K**. – "Because there is nobody around to look at me strange when I take 3000 photos of the same object."

**Tammy G.** – "When I was a kid I used to go with my parents to two cemeteries to care for graves of our loved ones. While my parents were busy cutting grass and such my brother and I would wander around the cemetery. I loved doing it, looking at the stones, being careful not to walk on any graves. Later on as a teen we would drive to various cemeteries and talk about local legends. (Every town has them.) (Which inspired me to write my book.) So now, I love the peace, the art and history. I wonder about those buried. I love being able to share and to see what others have to share. That's some of the reasons. … I think my parents did a fine job but what I didn't mention is when we went to cemeteries as teens, we were partying. Even still...we were always respectful."

**Dee M**. – "I started photographing cemeteries as an off-shoot of my genealogy. The more time I spent in cemeteries checking out the graves of my ancestors, the more I noticed how peaceful and beautiful they are. I don't think there is anywhere else in this world that you can find such heartfelt, artistic beauty as in a cemetery."

**Joe G.** - "Good question, Ed, it made me think.

1) Most cemeteries are beautiful places, by design, and the landscapes, the architecture, the sculptures all make such wonderful subjects, photographically.

2) I'm intrigued by the iconography of funereal sculpture and architecture.

3) The sense of history can be so strong, from the micro level of individual and inter-family relationships and life stories written on the headstones, up to the macro level of our own national history as you visit the graves of historical figures.

4) Cemeteries are such peaceful places to walk, meditate, see nature, and think about the human condition."

**Susan S**. – "I can remember always being afraid of cemeteries as a young girl. I don't know why, but I would hold my breath whenever we drove past a grave yard. Now I find myself drawn to them, finding peace and solace as I walk through those hollowed grounds. As many of you have stated, I too find myself thinking about the lives that once were, and are no more on this earth. Thus bringing to the forefront of my being, my own mortality. The difference between my childhood fears of death and all things related to it, and my peace and serenity of the same, is due to the eventuality of an acceptance of my own mortality. The knowing, in my own soul, that all is not finished when our lives on earth are done. There is more, much more ahead, just over yonder....."

**Anthony S**. – "I photograph cemeteries as a form of Memento Mori."

**Teresa R.** – "There's so much peace there, and the beauty of them I feel calm when I'm there and a closeness to my family."
John O'B. – "In 2005 I went to England. I went to many places including the British museum. To save weight I brought many memory cards instead of a computer. I toured the entire museum and took over 300 pictures. When I finally got home and looked at what I took I found. Gravestones, mummies, tombs and lot of funeral related stuff. So my tastes have been predetermined. I like graveyards and photograph them. Because I like it!"

**Johanna C**. – "As a kid (Youngest of 8) Cemeteries were my secret hiding spot from my family. Became fascinated by the statuary and the fact that someone took the time to handcarve/etch each one. I'd bring a drawing pad and a thermos of juice with me each day as I rode my bike to the nearest one. As an adult, I still visited the families stones that seemed abandoned and would tidy them up/plant flowers. Many years later I found out about findagrave.com and jumped right into it. They still are my favorite secret solitude away from home."

**Katie K**. – "Simple answer? Even at a young age I appreciated architecture and sculpture, but there is SO much of it. When I opened my eyes, as a teenager, to the sculpture in cemeteries, I discovered a way to narrow the field down and focus on a small subset of examples, which represented so many styles. Upon first learning about funerary symbolism, I knew I had found my niche. So, in essence, it was a matter of simply paring down my interests to what interested me the most. That, and, well, cemeteries are reflective of the communities they serve so it's a great way to get a quick local history lesson. … I didn't realize that was my process, Ed, until you asked the question and I really thought long and hard about it. So.... thanks for posing the question!"

**Dawn H.** – "Visiting a cemetery is like therapy to calm me. I have been doing it since I was a child. Photography came later after I discovered all the treasures that are held within them. I have never been to a cemetery where I didn't find something that was beautiful."

# CHAPTER 8:

# BEYOND THE HORIZON

After all this, I still cannot succinctly tell you why I spend time in cemeteries, or why I am so focused on death. Perhaps that is because there are many reasons – some that I am yet bound to discover.

# Burial at Sea

Originally published Wednesday, July 3, 2013
https://thecemeterytraveler.blogspot.com/2013/07/burial-at-sea.html

When it comes to the idea of "burial at sea," I'm probably influenced more by the romanticism of the idea than anything else. My guess is that most of my readers are too. When it comes to the cold, hard facts of how someone gets buried at sea, I'm in a rather wobbly boat. So it was with great interest and fascination that I phoned Captain Johnnie Lee, the proprietor of Long Beach, California's "Burials at Sea" service.

Amidst the pleasure cruise docks, tourist traps, and the Queen Mary in Long Beach, California, is an interesting sign on Pine Street's Dock 5: "Burials at Sea, by Captain Johnnie Lee (310) 387-0587." I was in Long Beach a couple weeks ago, so I went down to the docks and phoned Captain Lee. Unfortunately, he was not at his boat at the time, so I only conducted a phone interview with him. He was very forthcoming with his information, and after I told him I'd like to interview him for my Cemetery Traveler blog, he invited me to the boat the next day. Unfortunately, I was in the midst of a teaching engagement at the Convention Center and so had very limited time.

The idea of burial at sea is intriguing to me, so I had many questions about it. What you see below is as close as I can get to a transcript of our conversation. I took notes while sitting on the pier across from his boat (or rather, his yacht, the "Great Faith") on a sunny Saturday afternoon in June, 2013.

After I returned home to Philadelphia and read up on the subject, I found this notation from Captain Lee's website (http://www.burials-at-sea-by-captain.com/about-burials-at-sea-by-captain-lee.shtml). I'll let it set the stage for the interview:

Book of Revelations, Chapter 20, Verse 13:
*"And the Sea gave up her dead that were in it...."*

**Interview with Captain Johnnie Lee of "Burials at Sea"**

CT: How many burials do you do?
JL: Three or four families per day on the weekend, and maybe one or two during the week. I've been doing this for about fifteen years. My business has grown to approximately 400 services annually.

CT: I assume we're talking about ashes, not whole bodies?
JL: Correct. I do not do full body burials, just cremains. For full body burial, you have to go further out and you must be in at least 600 feet of water. You must also weigh the body down.

CT: How far out to sea do you go?
JL: Two to three miles – the law requires a minimum of five hundred yards.

CT: I hadn't thought of that - there are laws and regulations ...
JL: I am certified and licensed, as well as registered with the state [California Cemetery and Funeral Bureau] Cemetery Bureau.

*I should note that my interview was done right off the top of my head. I called Captain Lee spur-of-the-moment, and I truly appreciate his graciousness and patience with me. So my questions kind of jumped all over the place, often being spurred in a new direction based on unexpected information imparted to me by Captain Lee.*

CT: I assume your burials are somber events?
JL: Not really, it's not sad. It's peaceful, tranquil. The ocean helps a lot.

CT: How do you actually drop the ashes into the sea?
JL: I lower them into the ocean in a basket covered with red rose petals. When the last of the petals have floated away, I bring the basket back up.

CT: Sort of analogous to lowering a casket into the ground.
JL: Not really. It's a scattering at sea.

CT: It seems romantic, something I don't remember seeing anywhere on the East Coast.
JL: It's not so much romantic – scattering at sea is part of the Asian, Indian, Hindu, and Buddhist culture, but is becoming widely accepted by all people.

CT: For others, whose religion does not dictate a water burial, it seems like there is no actual closure, no tangible memory left of the deceased – no grave to visit.
JL: The event is one of release and tranquility; each one is unique. I give each family an 8 1/2" X 11" certificate that has a seascape in the background, with their loved one's name, date the service was performed, GPS coordinates of the exact burial site, and my signature.

*Captain Lee added, in a later conversation, "One of the advantages of a burial at sea service versus the traditional, is you don't have to wait for business hours to go visit your loved ones. Just go to the ocean, anywhere near the ocean, and you can have that closeness."*

CT: Do you get repeat business?
JL: Oh, yes many people who go out with me decide right then, that they want this type of service for themselves.

CT: Do you have any extraordinary recollections from your years of providing this service?
JL: Weather conditions. Choppy seas. On my first service, I let the surviving family member release the ashes overboard and the wind blew

them back at us. Since then, I designed the basket approach.

**End of Interview**

I have to say that Captain Lee in no way thought this final comment humorous – he was very serious and treated the matter with the utmost respect. The honor and dignity afforded to the process and people involved by Captain Lee was quite obvious. My interview ended there with his invitation to meet me at his boat the next day. Unfortunately I could not do this.

One of the intriguing questions regarding a burial at sea service would be, "How much does it cost?" Not something at all touched upon by Jessica Mitford, in her 1963 expose of the funeral industry, *The American Way of Death* (Simon and Shuster). You can view Captain Lee's full fee schedule from his Burials at Sea website (http://www.burials-at-sea-by-captain.com/), all of which seem quite reasonable. Prices range from one hundred dollars for a non-witnessed scattering to five hundred dollars for a witnessed burial at sea, for up to six people aboard his vessel, the "Great Faith" (a 48ft LOA Sea Ray Express Bridge Cruiser yacht).

Client families are required to obtain a Burial At Sea Permit from their mortuary, crematory or local Department of Health, and bring it with them on the day of the scattering. Captain Lee executes and files the Department of Health Permit with the appropriate agencies, with copies to the client and mortuary.

# Colma Cemeteries and Points Beyond

Originally published Saturday, April 16, 2011
https://thecemeterytraveler.blogspot.com/2011/04/colma-cemeteries-and-points-beyond.html

As I come to the end of my broadcast day, I thought I would share this last blog with you. It seemed appropriate as a concluding, bookend essay because it shows where "cemetery travel" can lead. This penchant I have for "dark tourism" may not exactly have been a pearl handed to me, but more of a net that's appeared after I made the leap into the unknown. California in the Spring of 2008, I spent some time shooting the cemeteries of Colma (a southern suburb of San Francisco). Yes, I know – normal people would visit Fisherman's Wharf or the Golden Gate, but Colma is a wonderful place if you do cemetery photography. I made it a point to shoot at the edges of the day, since that's when you get the best shadows, the best depth effect for black and white images. The first day I shot in the afternoon, the second in the morning.

Colma is a city of cemeteries – San Fran's official cemetery, in fact – truly a city of the dead. Unlike New Orleans, Colma's dead population outnumbers its living by a thousand to one! Within the town's two square miles are 18 cemeteries – 17 for humans and one for pets. The city's live population consists of about 1500 people (2010 census) while its dead number 1.5 million. Certain notables are buried here, including William Randolph Hearst, Wyatt Earp, Vince Guaraldi, and Joe DiMaggio. However, what really interested me in Colma was the Poole monument at Cypress Lawn Cemetery (Jennie Roosevelt Poole was a cousin of president Theodore Roosevelt.). This weeping angel (seen at the beginning of this essay) captured my interest ten years before when I first saw a photo of it in Douglas Keister's book, Going Out in Style. Its beauty enthralled me, and as I would be in the area, I had to see it in person.

Though I visited several cemeteries in Colma during my two-day stay, my sights were set primarily on the Poole monument. The statue itself did not disappoint, though it was difficult to photograph. This beautiful white marble sculpture is on a hill of sorts, and I could have used a stepladder to get a better angle. Also, the first day I was there, the weather was a bit dismal and there were sprinklers on near the statue! That's a drawback with these lovely well-maintained garden cemeteries. The first day I also photographed in nearby Hoy Sun Ning Yung Cemetery and The Italian Cemetery. I planned my return the next morning in an attempt to photograph the Poole angel, sans sprinklers. (You don't think Ansel Adams got that shot of Half Moon Dome on his first visit to Yosemite, do you?)

That first day, I found the Italian Cemetery to be a marvelous place, full of wonderfully detailed monuments. It's really your best bet for close-up work. The following day, I spent many hours at Cypress Lawn and Holy Cross Cemeteries, Colma's two largest. They're essentially across the street from each other – or rather, across the El Camino Real. Everything around here is so steeped in history, it gives you a feeling of limitless creativity. As writer Christopher Buckley says about California, "You can be anything you want to there as long as you don't mind being stuck in traffic."

Now, you wouldn't think two square miles of cemeteries is a lot of ground to cover. However, after two half-days, I was only able to visit the few I mentioned. In addition to the Poole monument, Cypress Lawn is as close as you'll get to an east coast Victorian garden cemetery, with its grand sweeping vistas, large monuments, ornate mausoleums, and a columbarium that left me utterly speechless. Holy Cross, the first of Colma's cemeteries

(1887), was the initial recipient of the mass exodus of dead San Franciscans when that city decided to move all its cemeteries outside the city limits. Holy Cross features a Googie-inspired receiving chapel (which must be seen to be believed) and a community mausoleum that was featured in the 1971 cult movie classic, Harold and Maude. Surrounding these imposing structures are 300 acres of densely packed religious iconography – so many angels that, as Mark Twain would say, you couldn't swing a cat without hitting one.

And speaking of Twain, back in 1866, he wrote a letter to Nevada's Territorial Enterprise newspaper, in which he levied this strong opinion about San Francisco cemeteries (I wonder if Jessica Mitford, in researching her 1963 expose of the death industry, *The American Way of Death* (Simon and Shuster), ever came across this??):

*"A prominent firm of undertakers here own largely in Lone Mountain Cemetery and also in the toll-road leading to it. Now if you or I owned that toll-road we would be satisfied with the revenue from a long funeral procession and would "throw in" the corpse – we would let him pass free of toll – we would wink placidly at the gate-keeper and say, "Nevermind this gentleman in the hearse – this fellow's a dead-head." But the firm I am speaking of never do that – if a corpse starts to Paradise or perdition by their road he has got to pay his toll or else switch off and take some other route. And it is rare to see the pride this firm take in the popularity and respectability of their cemetery, and the interest and even enthusiasm which they display in their business."* – Mark Twain

As a result of the Gold Rush of 1849, many saw California as the land of opportunity and flocked to Sacramento and San Francisco. By the late 1800s, the latter was becoming so developed that its government leaders decided the land was too valuable to be wasted on the dead. In 1900, the City and County of San Francisco passed an ordinance that there were to be no more burials allowed in San Francisco. In 1914, eviction notices were sent to all San Francisco cemeteries to remove human remains and monuments. The little town of Colma right next door inherited the bodies. Many went into mass graves if relatives could not pay the ten dollars for removal. (https://www.colma.ca.gov/colma-history/)

San Fransisco's cemeteries were closed, with a parade of hundreds of thousands of bodies headed for Colma. Colma became San Fransisco's official burial ground. Many monuments and tombstones from the original cemeteries were dumped into San Francisco Bay, lost souls forever forgotten.

But back to my photographic travels. My second day plan was to do a morning shoot in Holy Cross and Cypress Lawn (hopefully capturing the Poole Angel without the sprinkler) then a departure for other photographic pursuits. I did manage to get some reasonable images of the Poole Angel that day (the one you see above is about the best I could get), although Keister did it better. (In emulating the masters, we learn from them.) Afterward, I wanted to head south to Carmel and Point Lobos, near Big Sur, to shoot not stone angels, but another kind of stone on the rocky coast. Before I became interested in shooting cemetery statuary, I was a nature photographer. In this prior life, I loved shooting landscapes and such, but when I moved from upstate New York to Philadelphia, I found no nature there! (It was there all along, actually, I just had a hard time finding it.) I was photographically stalled for years. All that said, it wasn't necessarily the California landscape that drew me, but rather the aura of photographer Edward Weston.

Carmel, California is about 130 miles south of San Fran, which I allowed 3 hours to reach. Unfortunately, that was barely adequate, given the traffic through Santa Cruz. The scenery was breathtaking, even at high speed – the landscape had the true coloration of an Edward Hopper painting. By the time I blasted through Monterey, it was late in the day. Some other time, Seventeen Mile Drive – I needed to check in at the Weston Gallery before hitting the beach, Weston Beach, that is – black rocks, movie stars. Weston Beach, as they now call it, is at Point Lobos State Reserve, a couple miles south of Carmel, just above Big Sur.

Edward Weston, one of my photographer idols, lived and photographed in Carmel in the 1930s. He kind of lived life in the fast lane, but then most great artists live on the fringes of society. (I'll bet not many people know that one of the medium's heavyweights, Robert Frank, was the photographer and filmmaker of the Rolling Stones' most infamous unreleased film masterpiece, Cocksucker Blues.) The Weston Gallery is actually run by Weston's family. So a visit to the gallery is sort of like vicariously spending time with Weston himself. (As an aside, one of the items in which I take great pride is my rejection letter from the Weston Gallery, from when I sent them some of my cemetery photography back in the early 1990s.)

Carmel-by-the-Sea could never be confused with North Jersey's Avon-by-the-Sea (tho I love them both dearly) – it's more like Aspen, Colorado, a high-end retail resort. But you can ignore all that and enjoy the Weston Gallery, the pearl of the town. The gentleman running the gallery was very friendly, despite the fact that he knew I wasn't going to plunk down ten grand for a Weston print. When I eventually told him I was headed for Point Lobos, he said, "You'd better hurry, fog's going to be rolling in soon." Panic. Run! Drive fast! Bear in mind last visit to CA when you almost pancaked the rental T-Bird into stalled traffic on the PCH.

One of Weston's passions was photographing the stones at a particular beach at Point Lobos. Sounds absurd, but then, you never saw such stones. I'd seen the photos, and was intrigued, but I was totally unprepared for what this place looks like in real life. It's like another planet. I'm not sure such rock formations exist anywhere else on earth. And it all looks so fragile, weirdly eroded smooth rock held together by sandy grit. How could this all not just wash away? (Search the internet for images Edward Weston made at Point Lobos for examples.)

Weston Beach is within Point Lobos State Reserve. A couple miles south of Carmel, you come upon the park entrance. You drive maybe a mile through the woods to the Pacific, where you can get out and walk around. I got there toward the end of the day, and the air was misty. I shot some digital images, but felt that was a bit sacrilegious. The light was too dim to use my Holga, so I shot a roll of 35mm slide film. I walked around for about two hours, photographing here and there, mostly taking in the ambiance of the place. As the light faded, I thought about Weston shooting at the edges of the day. I was torn between spending this last hour of daylight either soaking it all in, or trying to capture it in photographs.

Toward the end, I felt a bit of what Weston must have felt every day he was there, when the light faded to the point where you could no longer photograph. I think it was the closest thing to a religious experience I've ever had in my life, feeling as he must have felt amidst this stunning natural beauty. You want to make hundreds of photographs of the rocks, try to capture the limitless abstract shapes and details. But then heaven's curtain begins to close on you. I wonder if Weston ever felt he truly captured the images for which he strived so hard? I think it's a bit like the feeling I had of not getting the perfect shot of the Poole Angel. So close to elation, but never attaining it – like searching for the Grail. As the fog slowly enveloped everything, it was time to release the doves and go home.

# ABOUT THE AUTHOR

Ed Snyder has been making photographs since the late 1970s, and began unleashing them on an unsuspecting public in 1982, through the Phoenix Street Gallery in New York. Since moving to Philadelphia in 1984, he has exhibited his work in many galleries. His work resides in public, private, and corporate collections. He is a member of the Photographic Society of Philadelphia, the Plastic Club, and the DaVinci Art Alliance.

Mr. Snyder has been a biomedical engineer since 1979, and has published extensively in that discipline. From 1986 through 2015, he worked at a university hospital in Philadelphia, where he was involved in the research, development, and clinical application of advanced cardio-pulmonary life support for babies ("ECMO"). With cemetery photography, then, his interests literally run from cradle to grave. The bridge? No matter how disparate medicine and art may appear, there is a connectedness – neither is considered a science, yet there is a precision to each, borne of technology, that is necessary for its success.

He has authored two books besides this one:

*Stone Angels* (Blurb) and *Digital Photography for the Impatient* (Amazon)

http://www.blurb.com/b/574773-stone-angels

https://www.amazon.com/Digital-Photography-Impatient-Ed-Snyder/dp/1448648270

*"As always your blog is fantastic and a pleasure to read! I admire your passion for the topic which we share."* – Martin S.

Made in the
USA
Middletown, DE

74131574R00078